Westminster Systematics

Westminster Systematics

Comments and Notes on the Westminster Confession

DOUGLAS WILSON

canonpress
Moscow, Idaho

Westminster Systematics: Comments and Notes on the Westminster Confession by Douglas Wilson

Westminster Systematics copyright © 2014 by Canon Press,
P. O. Box 8729, Moscow ID 83843 800-488-2034 | www.canonpress.com

Cover design by James Engerbretson.
Cover detail illustrations by Forrest Dickison.
Interior design by Valerie Anne Bost.

Unless otherwise noted, scripture quotations are from the King James Version.

Library of Congress Cataloging-in-Publication Data is forthcoming and will be available at www.canonpress.com.
ISBN-10: 1-59128-177-6
ISBN-13: 978-1-59128-177-1

16 17 18 19 20 21   10 9 8 7 6 5 4 3 2

To Tim Edwards,
for doing what needs to be done

CONTENTS

UNIT ELEVEN

UNIT TWELVE

UNIT THIRTEEN

UNIT FOURTEEN

APPENDIX

PREFACE
Introduction to Systematic Theology

We must always remember that a systematic understanding of any given text is really synonymous with a formal understanding of the text. Understanding a work is impossible unless there is an ability to summarize it, and summary is nothing but a systematic distillation. The real enemy to avoid is systematic *misunderstanding* of the text (not to mention systematic *misapplications*).

Another danger would be a correct systematic understanding of the text which is divorced from any living knowledge of the text. Imagine a student who had read the Cliff's Notes or Barnes Notes for a work of literature multiple times, but had never read the work itself. His knowledge would be accurate, but still *barren*.

So in our study of systematic theology, we are not striving for originality. We want to add our voices to those of the historic Church, so in this study we are going to follow (albeit not at every point) the Westminster Confession of Faith.

If you ever have occasion to look at the Constitution for the Communion of Reformed Evangelical Churches (CREC) you will find in the Preamble to that document a section that is perhaps a little bit unusual:

With patterns of church order and confessional standards, one of the fundamental requirements of Scripture is honesty (Ex. 20:16). Consequently, in the name of the Lord Jesus Christ, we charge you, the generations who will follow us in this confederation, to submit to the Scriptures with sincere and honest hearts, and to the standards of this confederation as consistent with the teaching of Scripture. When a portion of our order and confession is found to be out of conformity to Scripture, we charge you to amend it honestly, openly, and constitutionally, as men who must give an account to the God who searches the hearts of men. We charge you in the name of the Lord to abhor all forms of ignoring our intentions in what we have set down through dissembling, reinterpretation, dishonesty, relativism, pretended explanations, presumed spiritual maturity, assumed scholarly sophistication, or outright lying, so that the living God will not strike you and your children with a curse. We charge you to serve Him in all diligence and honesty, so that the blessings of the covenant may extend to your children for a thousand generations.[1]

Now was that quite necessary? Actually, yes, and here are some of the reasons. As Isaiah was a man of unclean lips, and dwelt among a people of unclean lips, so also for more than a century, Americans have been a people of dishonest subscription, and we dwell among a people of dishonest subscription. We evidence this in many ways, our treatment of the U.S. Constitution being a prime example. But the Church always leads the way, whether for good or ill. Christians were messing around with the Bible and with their respective confessions and statements of faith well in advance of the major distortions of our civil jurisprudence.

---

1   Communion of Reformed Evangelical Churches, "Constitution and By-Laws of the Communion of Reformed Evangelical Churches," Revised October 2011, http://www.crechurches. org/documents/governance/CREC_Constitution_2011.pdf.

Here's how it works. We have confounded a high view of a document in theory and a high view of it in practice. We have confounded praise and obedience. What good is an affirmation of the inerrancy of Scripture if we can always slip off the point of obedience by claiming that we are operating with a "fill-in-the-blank" hermeneutic?

Suppose Mom tells Billy that he is under no circumstances to play with matches, but one day while she is out, he accidentally burns down the garage. While he is explaining himself, it will do no good for him to say that he heard her *say* "don't play with matches," but that he has been experimenting lately with a post-structural hermeneutic. This won't fly, even if the garage was indisputably a structure at one time.

An authoritative document requires all those under its authority to have, by definition, the same basic hermeneutic in their approach to that document. Otherwise, the authoritative document in question is just the Queen Mum on her ninety-second birthday, waving from the balcony. Without a shared hermeneutic, authority is meaningless. And since authority is the whole point, a shared hermeneutic is necessary.

I will go further. If you want to find out who really runs the joint, find out who you are not allowed to apply a creative hermeneutic to. Nobody gets to read Supreme Court decisions the way *they* read the Constitution. If, for example, our august justices decide that the right to keep and bear arms means that we don't really have the right to keep and bear arms at all, after a quick experiment you will readily ascertain that you don't get to read their decision taking away your right to keep and bear arms as meaning, actually, that you *do* get to keep and bear arms. And since you have come crashing up to the place where a simple grammatical/historical hermeneutic is required, and no funny business, you have identified your rulers.

This same truth about the necessity of a shared hermeneutic applies to subordinate authorities, and not just to Scripture. Subscription to a confession is like getting married. First, you take your vows, and then you keep them. I don't just have a responsibility to "subscribe"; I have a responsibility to obey after I have subscribed. First you promise, and then you keep the promise. Many evangelical inerrantists think that all we have to do is make the promise. Many pastors in confessional traditions think the only hurdle they have to clear is the presbytery exam at the start.

Above I used the phrase, "the same *basic* hermeneutic," which recognizes that the use of human language at all opens the door to reasonable differences of interpretation. Let everyone be convinced in his own mind. But that elasticity, while always present to some degree, is not the fundamental principle. Different interpretations of authoritative documents are to be expected, and we should work charitably with our brothers and sisters to work through and resolve them. But cockamamie interpretations are also to be expected, and when that happens, somebody should say out loud that this is what has in fact happened.

For example, the Evangelical Theological Society has two simple requirements—a belief in the Trinity and a commitment to inerrancy. If the world were an honest place, this would be enough. But lest that inerrancy thing pinch all of us sinners too tightly, we can wiggle ourselves free by means of a "law/gospel hermeneutic," "a feminist hermeneutic," "a postmodern hermeneutic," "a post-garage hermeneutic," and so down the chute we all go.

Words are not infinitely elastic. The fact that there is always some room for honest discussion does not mean that there is all the room in the world. The closet is three by six, true enough, but the grand piano still can't go in there. Unless, of course, you have a post-structural hermeneutic, and come from a tradition where "closet" can refer to a pocket, and "piano" can mean harmonica.

I have argued before that liberals are sometimes more to be trusted with what Scripture actually says than are evangelicals. Because of the inerrancy thing, evangelicals are stuck with the results of their exegesis. Liberals can say Paul required women to refrain from teaching men, and that the husband is the head of the wife, ho, ho, ho, but the evangelical has to put on a magic hat that turns *kephale* into something more acceptable to the Academy, something like "trusted advisor." Frankly, it would be better if we evangelicals quit putting on the magic respectability hat and started putting on our big boy pants.

The same kind of thing can happen with subordinate standards, where Wesleyans might do a better job telling us what Westminster teaches than do the folks who don't want to be stuck with trying to explain how they have to agree with what they don't agree with. It doesn't matter what party or faction is being pinched by the words on the page—this is a *human* frailty, and not a failing of "those" other people over there. "Exhibit and confer" does not mean that nothing is conferred. "Effectual call" does not mean ineffectual call. "Keep and bear arms" means I can have a gun, and not that I can't.

So this is why those words are in the preamble to the CREC Constitution. We were talking to our sons and grandsons in a generation that is much given to this particular sin: "As evangelicals, we desire to confess the saving gospel of the Lord Jesus Christ in both love and doctrinal integrity." Words like this are always in season.

Just as we may speak to future generations, the generation that produced the Westminster Confession speaks to ours. From this distance, the Confession may seem like a serene exercise in systematic theological thought, produced back when they knew how to keep their libraries really quiet. But it is actually the serene product of a turbulent age.

The Westminster Assembly met from 1643 to 1652, the period of the English Civil Wars. Many of the political issues were also religious in nature, and had a direct impact on the work of the Assembly.

Anglicans tended to be royalists, siding with the king. Independents were with Cromwell, filling his magnificent army, and also exercising great influence in Parliament. Although the Westminster Assembly was formed by Parliament, and operated under its authority, the influence of Presbyterians was significant there.

The theological consensus was heavily Calvinistic, although the assembly was divided on questions of church government and other intramural reformational issues. Those interested in pursuing the historical and theological issues surrounding Westminster, could do no better than to seek out Robert Letham's wonderful book on the subject, entitled *The Westminster Assembly*. The subtitle is *Reading Its Theology In Historical Context*, and that exercise is most necessary and helpful in understanding the issues addressed in the Confession. All theological truth remains true, of course, and as C.S. Lewis said in another context, the square of the hypotenuse has not gone moldy from continuing to equal the sum of the square of the other two sides. But historical context still helps us understand why certain things were emphasized the way they were, and what particular doctrines meant in practical terms.

In a similar spirit, this volume has periodic readings in three other authors on related theological topics. This small book can certainly stand alone, but for the student who wants to pursue these topics more thoroughly, recommended readings in Francis Turretin, Thomas Vincent, and A.A. Hodge are found at the conclusion of each unit, with study questions connected to those readings. These authors hale from different places or eras, and can help the student see how these same topics were dealt with in different settings. Francis Turretin (1623–1687) lived in Geneva, serving both as a pastor and as a professor at the Academy of Geneva there. He was a precise Calvinistic thinker, but I repeat myself. Thomas Vincent (1634–1678) was an English Puritan, ministering during the tumultuous times which produced the Confession. He was a contemporary of Turretin, but much closer to the action. His work is a commentary on the Shorter Catechism, also a product of the Westminster Assembly. A.A. Hodge (1823–1886) was an American, teaching at the Old Princeton. He was the principal of Princeton Seminary from 1878 to 1886. The students at Princeton learned their theology from Turretin, until his work was replaced by the *Systematic Theology* of Charles Hodge, A.A. Hodge's father.

This book is intended for the theologically interested layman, as well an introduction to systematic theology for those students who are intending to pursue it further, up through their black belt. To both sorts of readers, I wish them the best of luck now, here in the Preface, because when they are done they won't believe in luck any more at all.

DOUGLAS WILSON
Christ Church
July 2014

UNIT ONE

CHAPTER 1
Of the Holy Scripture

We begin our discussion of how God has revealed Himself in His Word by looking at how He reveals Himself everywhere.

1. Although the light of nature, and the works of creation and providence do so far manifest the goodness, wisdom, and power of God, as to leave men inexcusable; (Rom. 2:14–15; 1:19–20; Ps. 19:1–3; Rom. 1:32; 2:1) yet they are not sufficient to give that knowledge of God, and of His will, which is necessary unto salvation (1 Cor. 1:21; 2:13–14). Therefore it pleased the Lord, at sundry times, and in divers manners, to reveal Himself, and to declare that His will unto His Church (Heb. 1:1); and afterwards, for the better preserving and propagating of the truth, and for the more sure establishment and comfort of the Church against the corruption of the flesh, and the malice of Satan and of the world, to commit the same wholly unto writing (Prov. 22:19–21; Luke 1:3–4; Rom. 15:4; Matt. 4:4, 7, 10; Isa. 8:19–20): which maketh the Holy Scripture to be most necessary (2 Tim. 3:15; 2 Pet. 1:19); those former ways of God's revealing His will unto His people being now ceased (Heb. 1:1–2).

Natural revelation, here called the "light of nature," provides enough rope for unconverted men to hang themselves. But in order for them to come to salvation, God must intervene, and He must do so with some sort of special revelation of Himself. In ancient times, He had done this in His own person and in various other ways. In later days, in order to make His Word more secure in the world—for both defensive and offensive purposes—He committed the way of salvation "wholly unto" writing. He also did this to protect His Church against the world, the flesh, and the devil. The Scriptures have entirely replaced God's former specific ways of revealing Himself in the world. This does not mean that Scriptures have replaced God's work in the world, but rather that we have been given a final and ultimate Word. God's general revelation, of course, continues as it did before.

2. Under the name of Holy Scripture, or the Word of God written, are now contained all the books of the Old and New Testament, which are these,

Of the Old Testament. Genesis, Exodus, Leviticus, Numbers, Deuteronomy, Joshua, Judges, Ruth, 1 Samuel, 2 Samuel, 1 Kings, 2 Kings, 1 Chronicles, 2 Chronicles, Ezra, Nehemiah, Esther, Job, Psalms, Proverbs, Ecclesiastes, The Song of Songs, Isaiah, Jeremiah, Lamentations, Ezekiel, Daniel, Hosea, Joel, Amos, Obadiah, Jonah, Micah, Nahum, Habakkuk , Zephaniah, Haggai, Zechariah, Malachi.

Of the New Testament. The Gospels according to Matthew, to Mark, to Luke, to John, the Acts of the Apostles, Romans, 1 Corinthians, 2 Corinthians, Galatians, Ephesians, Philippians, Colossians, 1 Thessalonians, 2 Thessalonians, 1 Timothy, 2 Timothy, Titus, Philemon, the Epistle to the Hebrews, the Epistle of James, the first and second Epistles of Peter, the first, second, and third Epistles of John, the Epistle of Jude, the Revelation of John.

All which are given by inspiration of God to be the rule of faith and life (Luke 16:29, 31; Eph. 2:20; Rev. 22:18–19; 2 Tim. 3:16).

The canonicity of the books of the Bible is a confessional issue for classical Protestants. These books, and not other books, are the only infallible and ultimate rule of faith and life. By faith, we mean *credenda*, those things which are to be believed. By life, we refer to *agenda*, those things which are to be done. In referring to these books of Scripture as the only infallible and ultimate rule of faith and life, this does not mean there are no other rules. It means there are no other *ultimate* and *infallible* rules.

Remember that the Table of Contents in your copy of the Bible was no more given by inspiration than were the maps, concordance, or ribbon. At the same time, they do represent an authoritative voice—that of the Church. But as we shall see in a moment, the Church's authoritative voice does not *make* anything Scripture. Rather, it is an uninspired recognition of that which already is inspired. To use Luther's example, John the Baptist pointed at Christ and declared Him to be the Lamb of God. This true testimony did not *make* Jesus the Lamb of God, but rather authoritatively recognized it. It is a similar case with the Church and the Scriptures.

The fact that the Church is a fallible authority does not mean that it has to get something wrong with everything. A fallible authority is capable of infallible testimony. I am certainly a fallible authority, and yet I can testify (infallibly) that two apples added to two other apples will always get you four apples. An infallible sentence, paragraph, or book can be created by a fallible author. Much more may a fallible authority infallibly collect and testify to an assemblage of God's utterances.

3. The books commonly called Apocrypha, not being of divine inspiration, are no part of the canon of the Scripture, and therefore are of no authority in the Church of God, nor to be any otherwise approved, or made use of, than other human writings (Luke 24:27, 44; Rom. 3:2; 2 Pet. 1:21).

This is not a rejection of the Apocrypha; it is a rejection of the Apocrypha as Scripture. The Apocrypha has many valuable things to teach us, but not with the authority of Scripture. This part of the Confession is an example of the Reformed cry *ad fontes*: "back to the sources." The Apocrypha comes to us courtesy of the Septuagint (LXX), and was not contained in the form of the Old Testament as it was used in Palestine. That is, it was not in the Bible that was used by Christ when He read the Scripture lesson in the synagogue. The Apocrypha as Scripture is part of the legacy of Hellenism and, as such, must be rejected. But the Apocrypha can and should be read for personal edification. There are things in there that are pretty silly, but most of it is better than most of what you can get in a modern Christian bookstore.

> 4. The authority of the Holy Scripture, for which it ought to be believed, and obeyed, dependeth not upon the testimony of any man, or Church; but wholly upon God (who is truth itself) the author thereof: and therefore it is to be received, because it is the Word of God (2 Pet. 1:19, 21; 2 Tim. 3:16; 1 John 5:9; 1 Thess. 2:13).

The Word of God is to be believed and obeyed because it is self-authenticating. Being what it is, how could it be otherwise? How could the authority of the Word depend upon another authority without that other authority taking the higher place? Men, whether individually or collectively, cannot be the source of divine authority. But there is an important qualification. Self-authenticating does not mean "authenticating to the individual self." Rather, it means that the authority resides within the text. That self-authoritative statement commends itself to the Church which, being the body of Christ, receives it gladly.

> 5. We may be moved and induced by the testimony of the Church to an high and reverend esteem of the Holy Scripture (1 Tim. 3:15). And the heavenliness of the matter, the efficacy of the

doctrine, the majesty of the style, the consent of all the parts, the scope of the whole (which is, to give all glory to God), the full discovery it makes of the only way of man's salvation, the many other incomparable excellencies, and the entire perfection thereof, are arguments whereby it doth abundantly evidence itself to be the Word of God: yet notwithstanding, our full persuasion and assurance of the infallible truth and divine authority thereof, is from the inward work of the Holy Spirit bearing witness by and with the Word in our hearts (1 John 2:20, 27; John 16:13–14; 1 Cor. 2:10–12; Isa. 59:21).

Does this mean that in praising the Scripture we offer no apologetic for the crucial role of the Church? Not at all. The authority of the Church may lawfully lead us to respect the Scriptures. The self-authentication of the Scriptures does not remove the various other arguments we may also consider for its inspiration. Rather, the self-authentication of the Bible is the basis for all such arguments. Arguments do not explain the way to the Word of God; the Word of God explains the way to the arguments. The Word of God is objectively what it is. But it cannot be seen for what it is unless the Holy Spirit illuminates the text. In accordance with His sovereignty, He may do this by various means. And, as it says here, the inward work of the Holy Spirit is done in our hearts. This is not a place that affirms a "just me and my Bible" approach.

6. The whole counsel of God concerning all things necessary for His own glory, man's salvation, faith and life, is either expressly set down in Scripture, or by good and necessary consequence may be deduced from Scripture: unto which nothing at any time is to be added, whether by new revelations of the Spirit, or traditions of men (2 Tim. 3:15–17; Gal. 1:8–9; 2 Thess. 2:2). Nevertheless, we acknowledge the inward illumination of the Spirit of God to be necessary for the saving understanding of such things as are

revealed in the Word (John 6:45; 1 Cor. 2:9–12): and that there are some circumstances concerning the worship of God, and government of the Church, common to human actions and societies, which are to be ordered by the light of nature, and Christian prudence, according to the general rules of the Word, which are always to be observed (1 Cor. 11:13–14; 14:26, 40).

If we need to know or do something of a spiritual nature, then God has told us in the Bible expressly what that is, or He has placed all the premises in the Scripture from which we may draw the necessary conclusions. We may not add anything necessary for God's glory, our salvation, or doctrine, or life on the basis of tradition or new revelation. Put simply, tradition and new revelation cannot bind the conscience. If someone tells you that in order to be saved, you must believe what the little voices in their head tell them to tell you, then you must walk away. "New revelation" does not trump what Scripture plainly teaches. In the same way, "old tradition" cannot be used to set aside the Word of God either.

At the same time, because men are sinners, inward and spiritual illumination is necessary to keep the Bible from being a closed book with regard to salvation. Although the Bible objectively teaches truth, it does not follow that dead men can read it. A man must be born again if he is to see the kingdom. He must be born again in order to really see the passages of Scripture that point to the kingdom.

Further, this paragraph in the Confession should not be taken as implying that we cannot make decisions concerning our worship and government based upon the light of nature and Christian prudence, provided such decisions are in general submission to the Word. How long should the service be? How should we configure or decorate the sanctuary? Go ahead and make your own decisions, the Westminster divines said. Just don't get crazy—which would rule out the junior high interpretive dance teams, not to mention the 500-pound thuribles.

7. All things in Scripture are not alike plain in themselves, nor alike clear unto all (2 Pet. 3:16): yet those things which are necessary to be known, believed, and observed for salvation, are so clearly propounded, and opened in some place of Scripture or other, that not only the learned, but the unlearned, in a due use of the ordinary means, may attain unto a sufficient understanding of them (Ps. 119:105, 130).

The Bible is not an esoteric book. There are hard places, but on the subject of salvation, the Scriptures taken as a whole are within reach of ordinary men. God did not give us the Bible to have something for seminarians to study. The Scriptures are the covenant document for *all* God's people.

8. The Old Testament in Hebrew (which was the native language of the people of God of old), and the New Testament in Greek (which, at the time of the writing of it, was most generally known to the nations), being immediately inspired by God, and, by His singular care and providence, kept pure in all ages, are therefore authentical (Matt. 5:18); so as, in all controversies of religion, the Church is finally to appeal unto them (Isa. 8:20; Acts 15:15; John 5:39, 46). But, because these original tongues are not known to all the people of God, who have right unto, and interest in the Scriptures, and are commanded, in the fear of God, to read and search them (John 5:39), therefore they are to be translated into the vulgar language of every nation unto which they come (1 Cor. 14:6, 9, 11–12, 24, 27–28), that, the Word of God dwelling plentifully in all, they may worship Him in an acceptable manner (Col. 3:16); and, through patience and comfort of the Scriptures, may have hope (Rom. 15:4).

The original is "authentical." This means the Hebrew of the Old Testament and the Greek of the New Testament. And this creates an interesting confessional issue—what of those small portions of the Old Testament which were written in Aramaic? It is common for people to take a trivial exception to the Confession at this point, but I don't think this is necessary. The New Testament calls Aramaic "Hebrew" in much the same way that we could call *The Canterbury Tales* "English."

These authentical writings were kept pure in all ages, which means that the WCF stands squarely against modern searches for the "original and historical text." Therefore, it is unconfessional to believe that the original text of Scripture was lost in the early centuries and then recovered over a millennium and a half later, as virtually all modern text criticism affirms. Not to put too fine a point on it, to follow modern textual criticism is to disagree with this portion of the WCF. Worse things have happened, of course, but historical honesty requires a man who uses (say) the UBS[2] text to take an exception to the WCF at presbytery.

At the same time, these authentical writings, which are the Word of God, are to be translated for the people of God into the vulgar tongues of all nations. Scripture in the original has a dual authority, both with regard to the substance—*quoad res*—and with regard to the words themselves—*quoad verba*. When they are translated, they retain their authority *quoad res*. But the final authority in controversies is the original. This is distinguished from the authority of ordinary teaching and preaching.

According to Westminster, the originals that were the final arbiter were the *apographic* texts, not the original autographs that nobody has. The *apographs* were the Word of God in both substance and words. The translations were the Word of God with regard to substance. The modern (and common) statement of faith that the Bible is inerrant in the autographs would have been considered by the men

---

2   The United Bible Society publishes a collated Greek text.

who drafted the Confession as hopelessly irrelevant. What good is an inerrant Bible that nobody has? You might as well affirm the inerrancy of the one copy of the Bible in heaven that Jesus uses.

> 9. The infallible rule of interpretation of Scripture is the Scripture itself: and therefore, when there is a question about the true and full sense of any Scripture (which is not manifold, but one), it must be searched and known by other places that speak more clearly (2 Pet. 1:20–21; Acts 15:15–16).

An obscure text is to be interpreted by plain texts, and not the other way around. The expositor should search for the one meaning of the text in question. The appeal here is to the true and full sense. The manifold sense (meaning the four layers of medieval interpretation called the *quadriga*) is to be rejected. According to the medieval hermeneutic, every text had a fourfold meaning:

1. the literal or historical meaning,
2. the tropological or moral meaning,
3. the allegorical or doctrinal meaning, and
4. the anagogical or ultimate eschatological meaning.

The rejection of this system of interpretation does *not* necessitate a rejection of these various kinds of meanings in various parts of the Bible; it is a rejection of this as an *a priori* system in approaching any given text.

This approach is not a rejection of allegory or typology which may be the sense of a particular place. It is a rejection of the allegorical method, which assumed all texts had the same four sedimentary layers of meaning. This part of the confession does not exclude complex meanings or require that every meaning be simple. In addition, the tropological meaning is often found in *application*, which is quite a different exercise than exegesis.

10. The supreme judge by which all controversies of religion are to be determined, and all decrees of councils, opinions of ancient writers, doctrines of men, and private spirits, are to be examined, and in whose sentence we are to rest, can be no other but the Holy Spirit speaking in the Scripture (Matt. 22:29, 31; Eph. 2:20; Acts 28:25).

The standard of *sola Scriptura* sets up Scripture as the supreme judge. This no more destroys lesser spiritual authorities than the existence of the Supreme Court excludes the existence of lower courts. Those entities, which have true spiritual authority and which may come under scriptural review, are conciliar decrees, ancient fathers, the teaching of Brother Love on TBN, and just me and my Bible. Notice that the supreme judge is the person of God, the Holy Spirit, as He speaks in and through Scripture.

Unit One: For Further Study

▨ Reading Assignments

A.A. Hodge, *The Confession of Faith*, pp. 1–45, 420–426 [Introduction, Chapter 1, Appendix 2]

Thomas Vincent, *The Shorter Catechism*, pp. v–xii, 13–26, 234–241 [Epistle to the Reader, To the Masters and Governors…, To the Young Ones…, Questions 1–3, 89–90]

Francis Turretin, *Institutes of Elenctic Theology*, Vol. 1 (Phillipsburg, NJ: P&R Publishing, 1992), pp. 98–116, 123–130 [Second Topic: Questions 8–11, 13–14][3]

▨ Questions on Reading

1. According to Hodge, to what extent can "Creeds and Confessions" bind the consciences of men?

2. What are the limits placed on the Church when it comes to making conditions of membership?

3. What is Hodge's argument for the canonical list for Old Testament books as received by Protestants?

---

3 Throughout this book, assigned page numbers refer to the following editions of the supplementary texts:

    A.A. Hodge, *The Confession of Faith* (Carlisle, PA: Banner of Truth, 1958).

    Thomas Vincent, *The Shorter Catechism* (Carlisle, PA: Banner of Truth, 1980).

    Francis Turretin, *Institutes of Elenctic Theology*, Volumes 1–3 (Phillipsburg, NJ: P&R Publishing, 1992).

If you are using different editions, the information in brackets will direct you to the correct sections of the texts.

4. What is the first argument that Vincent appeals to in showing that the Scriptures are the Word of God?

5. What is the difference in how Christ is revealed in the Old and the New Testaments?

6. What would make the Church an infallible authority, according to Vincent?

7. What love must we have in reading and hearing the Scriptures?

8. According to Turretin, does the Old Testament still serve as a canon of faith and rule of practice?

9. For Turretin, what are the touchstone languages for interpreting Scripture?

10. Did Turretin hold that the Septuagint was authentic?

UNIT TWO

CHAPTER 2
Of God, and of the Holy Trinity

We began with Scripture, not because the Bible is more important than God, but rather because we need to know how we can know about God—and this means we need to know where He speaks. But we now come to consider the nature, character, and attributes of God Himself.

> 1. There is but one only (Deut. 6:4; 1 Cor. 8:4, 6), living, and true God (1 Thess. 1:9; Jer. 10:10) . . .

Not that this should be necessary to say, but the Christian faith is monotheistic. The living and true God is the one who made Heaven and earth, of whom the Christian faith testifies, and within whom the Christian faith operates, along with everything else in the universe.

> . . . who is infinite in being and perfection (Job 11:7–9; 26:14) . . .

When we say that God is infinite, we are simply saying He is *not* finite. He is not finite or limited in His essence, or in the perfection of His attributes. We have no clear positive notion of what we mean by *infinite*, because we are finite creatures. But we do know that God is not like us.

> ...a most pure spirit (John 4:24), invisible (1 Tim. 1:17), without body, parts (Deut. 4:15–16; John 4:24; Luke 24:39), or passions (Acts 14:11, 15)...

God's being is spiritual, not material, and He cannot be seen. When it is said that He is without body, parts, or passions, this refers to God's simplicity. He is not a complicated, tangled knot of attributes. There is no contradiction within the Godhead between this attribute and that one. But we have to be careful with the truth that He is without "passions." If this is handled or stated wrongly, it can make the orthodox position vulnerable to the charge of abstractionism. His passion is not like a man's passion—a temper tantrum. But neither is it like a calm summer day. His anger is far more terrible than man's anger. His anger would be trans-passionate, not sub-passionate. The divine wrath is not a block of ice.

> ...immutable (James 1:17; Mal. 3:6), immense (1 Kings 8:27; Jer. 23:23–24), eternal (Ps. 90:2; 1 Tim. 1:17), incomprehensible (Ps. 145:3), almighty (Gen. 17:1; Rev. 4:8), most wise (Rom. 16:27), most holy (Isa. 6:3; Rev. 4:8), most free (Ps. 115:3), most absolute (Exod. 3:14)...

God cannot change or be changed. He is boundless and immense. He is eternal, which is not the same as everlasting. Eternity refers to a trans-temporal existence. A finite head cannot contain the truth about God; He is incomprehensible. If He could be comprehended by us, He would not be worthy of our worship. He has all power, but this power is not disconnected from wisdom. His holiness is the confluence of all His attributes, just as white is the combination of all colors. He is free, not constrained by anything other than His own nature and attributes. He is the standard by which anything and everything else is to be judged.

. . . working all things according to the counsel of His own immutable and most righteous will (Eph. 1:11), for His own glory (Prov. 16:4; Rom. 11:36) . . .

God has a plan for everything He does, and what He does encompasses everything. He works out all details according to His master plan. The *telos* behind all that He determines to do is His own glory.

. . . most loving (1 John 4:8, 16), gracious, merciful, long–suffering, abundant in goodness and truth, forgiving iniquity, transgression, and sin (Exod. 34:6–7); the rewarder of them that diligently seek Him (Heb. 11:6); and withal, most just, and terrible in His judgments (Neh. 9:32–33), hating all sin (Ps. 5:5–6), and who will by no means clear the guilty (Nah. 1:2, 3; Exod. 34:7).

The world is a display case for many of God's attributes, and this explains why He permitted evil to come into the good world He created. In a world without sin, God's mercy and justice would have gone unrevealed. As this is obviously intolerable, God determined to create a world in which sinners would rebel against Him, some of them receiving mercy and others justice. Those who receive mercy understand that He is most loving and gracious. They see His patience, and the abundance of His kindness, including His willingness to put away sin and iniquity. Further, His goodness is shown in how He rewards those who seek Him. At the same time, His justice is plainly in evidence with others. He is terrible and hates sin (not to mention the sinner). In no way can God be brought to clear the guilty.

2. God hath all life (John 5:26), glory (Acts 7:2), goodness (Ps. 119:68), blessedness (1 Tim. 6:15; Rom. 9:5), in and of Himself; and is alone in and unto Himself all-sufficient, not standing in need of any creatures which He hath made (Acts 17:24–25), nor deriving any glory from them (Job 22:2–3) . . .

God is self-sufficient. He is a sun, not a moon. He reflects nothing, but rather is the eternal fountainhead of all these attributes, which are then reflected by all things that have been created. He is the source of all life, glory, goodness, and blessedness. He did not create us because He was lonely, which is a crucial point. He created all things to glorify Himself, but this does not mean He needed glory, or somehow was lacking in it. An infinite Being, He is the source of infinite surplus.

> ... but only manifesting His own glory in, by, unto, and upon them.

His glory is manifested in the world, but not made possible by the world.

> He is the alone fountain of all being, of whom, through whom, and to whom are all things (Rom. 11:36); and hath most sovereign dominion over them, to do by them, for them, or upon them whatsoever Himself pleaseth (Rev. 4:11; 1 Tim. 6:15; Dan 4:25, 35).

As the Lord of all creation, His right of disposal is absolute. All things flow from Him, and all things have their meaning and value in reference to Him. Being who He is, He may consequently do whatever He feels like doing. Our God is in heaven; He does as He pleases.

> In His sight all things are open and manifest (Heb. 4:13), His knowledge is infinite, infallible, and independent upon the creature (Rom. 11:33–34; Ps. 147:5), so as nothing is to Him contingent, or uncertain (Acts 15:18; Ezek. 11:5).

God's knowledge is not mediated to Him in any way, or by any means. God learns nothing. He in no way troubleshoots the created order, going first this way, then that. Nothing stands between God and what He knows. All things are certain to Him. He has no epistemological difficulties.

He is most holy in all His counsels, in all His works, and in all His commands (Ps. 145:17; Rom. 7:12). To Him is due from angels and men, and every other creature, whatsoever worship, service, or obedience He is pleased to require of them (Rev. 5:12–14).

The fact that God's power over the creation is absolute does not mean that He wields this power in unrighteousness. He works all things according to His counsel, but it must be remembered that His counsel is *holy*. Consequently, if God tells us to do something, it is holy and right for us to obey Him without question. This is to be distinguished from obeying without question something which someone falsely claims to be the Word of God. Apart from the Word of God, for a father to do to his son what Abraham did to Isaac would be most wicked.

3. In the unity of the Godhead there be three persons, of one substance, power, and eternity: God the Father, God the Son, and God the Holy Ghost (1 John 5:7; Matt. 3:16–17; 28:19; 2 Cor. 13:14):

When we confess the Trinity, we are confessing the tri-unity of the one God. One and three are not predicated of the same thing. One refers to the substance, power, and eternity of God, while three refers to the Persons within the Godhead, who each has all the same attributes of the one God. Each Person of the Trinity is eternal, meaning that the Trinity did not begin at a certain point but was mere Unity before that. The three Persons involved are revealed to us in Scripture as the Father, Son, and Holy Ghost.

. . . the Father is of none, neither begotten, nor proceeding;

The Father is the authority and source. But since He is eternally the source, the other two Persons are equally eternal, and eternally dependent upon the source. The Son is begotten, the Father is not.

The Spirit proceeds, the Father does not. The Father does not come from anywhere.

> . . . the Son is eternally begotten of the Father (John 1:14, 18);

To use the phrase applied to this by John the apostle, the Son is *monogenes*, the only-begotten. This is a technical term, referring to just this truth. In some places, Scripture refers to Christ as the first born from the dead, referring to the resurrection. But this passage here is referring to the eternal relationship of the Father to the Son.

> . . . the Holy Ghost eternally proceeding from the Father and the Son (John 15:26; Gal. 4:6).

The Westminster Confession follows the Western church, accepting the *filioque* clause which was inserted into the Nicean Creed, and which caused much trouble. But aside from how the clause came to be confessed, this particular confession remains sound. *The Spirit is in truth the Spirit of Christ, as well as the Spirit of the Father.*

Unit Two: For Further Study

▓ Reading Assignments

Hodge pp. 46–62 [Chapter 2]

Vincent, pp. 27–42 [Questions 4–6]

Turretin, Vol. 1, pp. 194–212, 253–272 [Third Topic: Questions 8–12, 23–25]

▓ Questions on Reading

1. According to Hodge, what relation does God as "personal spirit" have to the world?

2. In what way does Scripture condescend to our weakness in talking about God?

3. What does Hodge say about the nature of the one God?

4. What distinction does he make between attributes and properties?

5. According to Vincent, what is the wisdom of God?

6. Does Vincent think God can do absolutely anything?

7. Does Vincent say that the essence of God is the same in all three persons?

8. According to Turretin, where does the infinity of God "reside"?

9. For Turretin, do we have adequate vocabulary for talking about the ubiquity of God?

10. In what sense is the Trinity a fundamental article, and in what sense not?

UNIT THREE

CHAPTER 3
Of God's Eternal Decree

We now come to the place where the transcendental rubber meets the immanent road.

> 1. God from all eternity, did, by the most wise and holy counsel of His own will, freely, and unchangeably ordain whatsoever comes to pass (Eph. 1:11; Rom. 11:33; Heb. 6:17; Rom. 9:15, 18): yet so, as thereby neither is God the author of sin (James 1:13, 17; 1 John 1:5), nor is violence offered to the will of the creatures; nor is the liberty or contingency of second causes taken away, but rather established (Acts 2:23; Matt. 17:12; Acts 4:27–28; John 19:11; Prov. 16:33).

This paragraph describes what is usually called predestination, but should more properly be called foreordination. The word *predestination* is usually applied in Scripture to the surety that the elect (once regenerated) will come at last to the resurrection of the body. But the truth represented by the common use of this word is still sure: before the world was made, from all eternity, God decreed the number of hairs on that yellow dog's back. This is something He did in all wisdom. What was so decreed is settled, both freely and unalterably.

This was done in such a way that God cannot be charged with sin. This is of course true by definition (God cannot sin), but it is also important to reiterate the point. God is the Creator of a world which is now full of sin, and yet He cannot be charged with the guilt of it. This confession says that God ordains that sinful action y will take place, and yet He is not the author of sinful action y. Another position (Arminianism) holds that God foreknows sinful action y, and yet is not the author of it. Still another position says that God does not know the future, and created the world anyway despite the possibility of sinful action y (openness theism).

But if men can charge God with being implicated in evil, then they may with justice continue to charge Him as long as the doctrine of creation is affirmed at any level. There is no escape; if God is the Creator, then He is responsible for the presence of sinful action y. We might as well face it. If we have the authority to charge the Calvinist God with tyranny, then we also have the authority to charge the Arminian God with culpable negligence, and the openness god with being drunk and disorderly. Of course, as St. Paul would say, I am out of my mind to talk like this. But if God made the world, then He is responsible for it being here, and for it being in the condition it is in.

The only consistent position on this is the view that explicitly holds that God is exhaustively sovereign. All Christians who hold to *creatio ex nihilo* are Calvinists in principle. They hold to exhaustive sovereignty implicitly, but won't say so out loud, which leads to inconsistencies and contradictions. If anybody on the scene knows what is happening, hilarity ensues.

At the same time, this view does not make God the master puppeteer. What He foreordained was a world full of free choices. He not only ordained that a man would be in the ice cream store choosing one of thirty-one flavors, He also decreed which flavor would be chosen. But this is not all; He ordained that the cookie dough ice cream would be chosen by this man *freely*. God ordains non-coercively. This makes no sense to some people, but how many basic doctrines do make sense? We do not understand how God made Jupiter from nothing any more than how He determined my actions today without annihilating me. But He does. Remember, the point being made here is not that divine sovereignty is merely consistent with secondary freedom, but rather that it is the doctrine that *establishes* it.

> 2. Although God knows whatsoever may or can come to pass upon all supposed conditions (Acts 15:18; 1 Sam. 23:11–12; Matt 11:21, 23), yet hath He not decreed any thing because He foresaw it as future, or as that which would come to pass upon such conditions (Rom. 9:11, 13, 16, 18).

God does foreknow all things, and He knows all the possibilities and contingencies. He knows everything that could have been. And yet we are not to suppose that God foreordains based upon His knowledge of what the world would have done without Him anyway. He does not peer down the corridors of time, see what is happening, and then decree that it will happen. This would make God nothing more than a cosmic "me-too-er," which is incoherent. If God saw what was going on down the corridors of time without Him, and then created that world, then His decision to create the world means that those events were not going on without Him. He is the one who decreed that they would be.

> 3. By the decree of God, for the manifestation of His glory, some men and angels (1 Tim. 5:21; Matt. 25:41) are predestinated unto everlasting life; and others foreordained to everlasting death (Rom. 9:22–23; Eph. 1:5–6; Prov. 16:4).

God does what He does, by His decree, and for His glory. This includes the apportionment of everlasting life, both to men and angels. Some are predestined to life, while others are foreordained to everlasting death. The use of different verbs here is significant. God's predestination to life is assigned to men who are in a state of death. God's decision to leave someone in his death is different in substance from His decision to remove someone from that death. Consider ten men on death row, all of whom deserve to die. The governor, for good and sufficient reasons, decides to pardon three of them. Has he done an injustice to the other seven? His action *affects* all ten, but his action toward the three is of a different nature than his lack of action toward the seven. God is not selecting individuals for eternal bliss or eternal pain from some morally neutral place. We are all of us condemned sinners, and the election to life is an election to *pardon*.

> 4. These angels and men, thus predestinated, and foreordained, are particularly and unchangeably designed, and their number so certain and definite, that it cannot be either increased or diminished (2 Tim. 2:19; John 13:18).

This paragraph in the Confession simply keeps men from messing around with the words—which, on a subject like this, they frequently want to do. Because the word *predestination* is in the Bible, something must be done with it. But we are basically dealing with two lists of names, both of which are fixed. The lists do not grow or shrink, and names on the lists cannot be exchanged. God knows the end from the beginning.

> 5. Those of mankind that are predestinated unto life, God, before the foundation of the world was laid, according to His eternal and immutable purpose, and the secret counsel and good pleasure of His will, hath chosen, in Christ, unto everlasting glory (Eph. 1:4, 9, 11; Rom 8:30; 2 Tim. 1:9; 1 Thess. 5:9), out of His mere free grace and love, without any foresight of faith, or good works, or

perseverance in either of them, or any other thing in the creature, as conditions, or causes moving Him thereunto (Rom. 9:11, 13, 16; Eph. 1:4,9): and all to the praise of His glorious grace (Eph. 1:6, 12).

This is a fine statement of unconditional election, which is entirely different from arbitrary or capricious election. The truth being insisted upon here is that God has no reasons found in us for His election. He has many reasons, all of them good, for His selection. He does what He does according to His secret *counsel* and the *good* pleasure of His will. Further, the choice springs from His grace and love. This means that God has compelling reasons for election—it is not a question of *eeny, meeny, miney, moe.* But the good reasons do not include foresight of our faith, good works, stamina in either, or anything else that might be found in the creature which would enable that creature to boast in anything other than God's goodness and mercy.

> 6. As God hath appointed the elect unto glory, so hath He, by the eternal and most free purpose of His will, foreordained all the means thereunto (1 Pet. 1:2; Eph. 1:4–5; 2:10; 2 Thess. 2:13). Wherefore, they who are elected, being fallen in Adam, are redeemed by Christ (1 Thess. 5:9–10; Titus 2:14), are effectually called unto faith in Christ by His Spirit working in due season, are justified, adopted, sanctified (Rom. 8:30; Eph. 1:5; 2 Thess. 2:13), and kept by His power, through faith, unto salvation (1 Pet. 1:5). Neither are any other redeemed by Christ, effectually called, justified, adopted, sanctified, and saved, but the elect only (John 17:9; Rom. 8:28–39; John 6:64–65; 10:26; 8:47; 1 John 2:19).

If God has elected certain men to salvation, then why pray, preach, witness, etc.? The answer is that God does not just predestine the end, which is, for example, the salvation of Smith. He also predestined, as a necessary part of the whole process, the varied preconditions and means which were necessary to bring Smith to the point of salvation. These preconditions included being fallen in Adam, redeemed by Christ, and called and kept by the Holy Spirit. The elect have all the preconditions preordained for them, and those who are not elect do not participate in the foreordained salvific preconditions.

God does not just ordain the end; He ordains the means as well. If He ordains the harvest, He also ordained the plowing and planting. If He ordained the pregnancy, He ordained the sexual union. If He ordained the dent in the fender, He ordained the fender-bender that caused it. We cannot separate one small portion of an ordained universe and treat it in isolation, as though the rest of the universe were not that way. Let us at least learn simple logic from the pagan philosopher Zeno, founder of the Stoics. He caught a slave stealing, and gave him a good thrashing for it. The slave, an amateur philosopher himself, pleaded that it was fated for him to steal. And Zeno retorted, "And that I should beat you."

> 7. The rest of mankind God was pleased, according to the unsearchable counsel of His own will, whereby He extendeth or withholdeth mercy, as He pleaseth, for the glory of His sovereign power over His creatures, to pass by; and to ordain them to dishonour and wrath for their sin, to the praise of His glorious justice (Matt. 11:25–26; Rom. 9:17–18, 21–22; 2 Tim. 2:19–20; Jude 4; 1 Pet. 2:8).

If this is done according to the unsearchable counsel of His own will, then we should not try to search it out. We may assert it, because the Bible does, but cannot plumb the depths of His counsel at this point. God may withhold mercy without injustice. If mercy could be demanded as a matter of justice, then it would no longer be mercy. Mercy and grace can never be demanded as a right. Why does

God pass by some of His creatures, leaving them in their sin? He does this in order to manifest His justice, which is glorious. In order for justice to be manifested, it is necessary that sinners fall under dishonor and wrath. In a world without sin, two of God's most glorious attributes—His justice and His mercy—would go undisplayed. This, obviously, would be horrible. This is Paul's argument. What if God did this to show His wrath on the vessels of wrath, and to bestow the riches of His glory on the vessels of mercy (Rom. 9:22–23)?

> 8. The doctrine of this high mystery of predestination is to be handled with special prudence and care (Rom. 9:20; 11:33; Deut. 29:29), that men, attending the will of God revealed in His Word, and yielding obedience thereunto, may, from the certainty of their effectual vocation, be assured of their eternal election (2 Pet. 1:10). So shall this doctrine afford matter of praise, reverence, and admiration of God (Eph. 1:6; Rom. 11:32); and of humility, diligence, and abundant consolation to all that sincerely obey the Gospel (Rom. 11:5–6, 20; 2 Pet. 1:10; Rom. 8:33; Luke 10:20).

This truth should be handled gingerly. Sinners like to blame God instead of themselves, and they do so with particular impudence whenever they become aware of this truth. But the reason we emphasize it is threefold. First, we must understand this in order to make our calling and election sure. Secondly, it gives rise to many occasions where God may be greatly glorified.

Lastly, this doctrine is a real humbler. Those who are proud of their knowledge of this doctrine (as opposed to all those modern evangelical semi-Pelagians out there) have the worst of all situations. The most obvious thing about predestination is that it exalts God and abases the creature. But this is not be confused with the exaltation of the creature who pretends to exalt God. As John Newton memorably put it,

And I am afraid there are Calvinists, who, while they account it a proof of their humility that they are willing in words to debase the creature, and to give all the glory of salvation to the Lord, yet know not what manner of spirit they are of. Whatever it be that makes us trust in ourselves that we are comparatively wise or good, so as to treat those with contempt who do not subscribe to our doctrines, or follow our party, is a proof and fruit of a self-righteous spirit. Self-righteousness can feed upon doctrines, as well as upon works; and a man may have the heart of a Pharisee, while his head is stored with orthodox notions of the unworthiness of the creature and the riches of free grace.[4]

The Pharisee who went down to the Temple to pray actually began his prayer with one of the solas—*soli Deo gloria.* "I thank Thee, God . . ." Perfectly orthodox. And he went home unjustified to boot.

---

4   The Works of John Newton (Carlisle: Banner of Truth, 1985), 272.

Unit Three: For Further Study

Reading Assignments

Hodge, pp. 63–79 [Chapter 3]

Vincent, pp. 42–44 [Question 7]

Turretin, Vol. 1, pp. 311–322 [Fourth Topic: Questions 1–4]

Questions on Reading

1. According to Hodge, do the decrees of God include the sinful actions of men?

2. Which groups did not think that God could foresee the future actions of men?

3. What group does Hodge say grants the foreknowledge of God while denying foreordination?

4. Can God elect someone to salvation who is not in fact saved?

5. What distinction does Vincent make with regard to the decrees of God?

6. What does not factor into God's decrees of election and reprobation?

7. In what two ways does God fulfill His decrees?

8. According to Turretin, in what ways do the decrees of God *not* "inhere" in Him?

9. Who denies the eternity of the decrees?

10. Does God decree anything conditionally?

UNIT FOUR

CHAPTER 4
Of Creation

And so, where did this world come from anyhow?

> 1. It pleased God the Father, Son, and Holy Ghost (Heb. 1:2; John 1:2–3; Gen. 1:2; Job 26:13; 33:4), for the manifestation of the glory of His eternal power, wisdom, and goodness (Rom. 1:20; Jer. 10:12; Ps. 104:24; 33:5–6), in the beginning, to create, or make of nothing, the world, and all things therein whether visible or invisible, in the space of six days; and all very good (Gen. 1; Heb. 11:3; Col. 1:16; Acts 17:24).

What did God make? He made everything. When did He do this? He did it in the beginning, over the course of six days. These should be understood, naturally, as six *ordinary* days. Where did God create? The answer to this is everywhere. The reason He did this was to manifest His eternal power, wisdom, and goodness. How was all this accomplished? We do not know. Beats us. How would we know something like that? Who is the Creator God? The triune God has made all things. He is the Maker of Heaven and earth.

> 2. After God had made all other creatures, He created man, male and female (Gen 1:27), with reasonable and immortal souls (Gen. 2:7; Eccl. 12:7; Lk. 23:43; Matt. 10:28), endued with knowledge,

righteousness, and true holiness, after His own image (Gen. 1:26; Col. 3:10; Eph. 4:24); having the law of God written in their hearts (Rom. 2:14–15), and power to fulfill it (Eccl. 7:29): and yet under a possibility of transgressing, being left to the liberty of their own will, which was subject unto change (Gen. 3:6; Eccl. 7:29). Beside this law written in their hearts, they received a command, not to eat of the tree of the knowledge of good and evil (Gen. 2:17; 3:8–11, 23); which while they kept, they were happy in their communion with God, and had dominion over the creatures (Gen. 1:26, 28).

Mankind is created with two aspects, male and female. Men alone do not constitute mankind. Without women, mankind does not exist. Male and female created He them. We were created with reasonable souls, destined for life beyond this life. We have a contingent immortality, not an essential immortality—it is the gift of God. By this we mean that God gives us the gift of life, and our immortal souls have this life ordinarily by possession of a physical body. Christians do not so much hold to a doctrine of the "immortality of the soul," as much as to the doctrine of the resurrection of the dead.

The Bible tells us in the Old Testament that we bear the *imago Dei*, but the New Testament gives us a description of this image: knowledge, righteousness, and holiness. The Bible does *not* define the image of God as "reason." Angels are reasonable creatures and do not bear the image of God the same way we do. Handicapped humans might not be able to reason well, and yet they do bear the image of God. So what is the image? We have a true sense of right and wrong built in, God having written His law on the heart—it is knowledge, righteousness and true holiness. Because of sin, this image has been marred, and so we have to grow back into that image as we grow up into Jesus Christ. Our ability to be in union with Jesus in this way is the image of God.

When we were created, we had the true possibility of obedience, meaning that nothing in our nature hindered us in obeying. At the same time, being in a state of probationary innocence, we had the possibility of disobeying. In addition to an innate sense of right and wrong, God had also commanded us to refrain from eating from the tree of the knowledge of good and evil. Until we disobeyed Him in this, we were content in fellowship with God, and we had dominion over the beasts of the earth.

CHAPTER 5
Of Providence

God did not just make the world; He also governs it.

> 1. God the great Creator of all things doth uphold (Heb. 1:3), direct, dispose, and govern all creatures, actions, and things (Dan. 4:34–35; Ps. 135:6; Acts 17:25–26, 28; Job 38; 39; 40; 41), from the greatest even to the least (Matt. 10:29–31), by His most wise and holy providence (Prov. 15:3; Ps. 104:24; 145:17), according to His infallible foreknowledge (Acts 15:18; Ps. 94:8–11), and the free and immutable counsel of His own will (Eph. 1:11; Ps. 33:10–11), to the praise of the glory of His wisdom, power, justice, goodness, and mercy (Isa. 63:14; Eph. 3:10; Rom. 9:17; Gen. 45:7; Ps. 145:7).

God upholds everything. He directs everything; He disposes and governs every creature, every action, and every thing that is. This is something He does without diminishing or draining His power, whether the creature in question is a cluster of galaxies or a cluster of atoms. The hairs of our head are numbered. This He does in holiness and wisdom. His providence (for this is what we call it) is according to a foreknowledge that cannot be in error, and also according to His free and unalterable counsel. The reason He does this is so that His wisdom, power, justice, goodness, and mercy might be glorified. It follows that we should not whisper this doctrine or keep silent about it for fear that it might not glorify Him. Our fears for His glory are nothing compared to His zeal for His glory.

> 2. Although, in relation to the foreknowledge and decree of God, the first Cause, all things come to pass immutably, and infallibly (Acts 2:23); yet, by the same providence, He ordereth them to fall out, according to the nature of second causes, either necessarily, freely, or contingently (Gen 8:22; Jer. 31:35; Exod. 21:13; Deut. 19:5; 1 Ki. 22:28, 34; Isa. 10:6–7).

His providence determines that all things will come to pass; the end is known and cannot be changed. But that same providence also knows what will happen *causatively* the moment before. God oversees the end, but also the means. And His providence of the means is fully consistent with the nature of secondary causes: some things happen necessarily, like a rock tumbling in an avalanche. Other things happen freely, as when a man chooses to go left instead of right. Other things happen contingently, as when one thing depends upon another.

> 3. God, in His ordinary providence, maketh use of means (Acts 27:31, 44; Isa. 55:10–11; Hos. 2:21–22), yet is free to work without (Hos. 1:7; Matt. 4:4; Job 34:10), above (Rom 4:19–21), and against them (2 Ki. 6:6; Dan. 3:27), at His pleasure.

The fact that we have asserted that God uses means does not mean that we hold He is bound to use means. This would be to deny Him the power to work miracles. But He is the Lord, He dwells in the highest heaven, and He does as He pleases.

> 4. The almighty power, unsearchable wisdom, and infinite goodness of God so far manifest themselves in His providence, that

it extendeth itself even to the first fall, and all other sins of angels and men (Rom. 11:32–34; 2 Sam. 24:1; 1 Chron. 21:1; 1 Ki.
22:22–23; 1 Chron. 10:4, 13–14; 2 Sam. 16:10; Acts 2:23; 4:27–
28); and that not by a bare permission (Acts 14:16), but such as
hath joined with it a most wise and powerful bounding (Ps. 76:10;
2 Ki. 19:28), and otherwise ordering, and governing of them, in
a manifold dispensation, to His own holy ends (Gen. 50:20; Isa.
10:6–7, 12); yet so, as the sinfulness thereof proceedeth only from
the creature, and not from God, who, being most holy and righteous, neither is nor can be the author or approver of sin (James
1:13–14, 17; 1 John 2:16; Ps. 50:21).

What we have extended with the right hand, we do not take back
with the left. If God orders all things, then He orders *sin*. If He orders sin, then He ordered the sin of our first parents. Every sin ever
committed takes its perfect place in the plans and counsels of the
Almighty. As it has been well said, God draws straight with crook-
ed lines. God's determination that these sins would occur does not
occur by "bare permission," but He also bounds, orders, and governs
the sin to His own holy purposes. Notice that God does what He
does by means of permission, but it is not a *bare* permission; it is
permission accompanied. Despite this, and despite the demands of
our own sinful hearts, the guilt of any such sin adheres to the sinful
creatures only and not to Him who does not approve of it. He is the
author of the fact of the sin, the limits of the sin, the place of the
sin, the purpose of the sin, the meaning of the sin, but He is not the
author of the sin itself. He approves it, but He does not approve *of*
it. Judas was bound to betray the Lord, just as it was determined, but
the God who determined it was not the traitor—Judas was.

5. The most wise, righteous, and gracious God doth oftentimes
leave, for a season, His own children to manifold temptations,
and the corruption of their own hearts, to chastise them for their

former sins, or to discover unto them the hidden strength of corruption and deceitfulness of their hearts, that they may be humbled (2 Chron. 32:25–26, 31; 2 Sam. 24:1); and, to raise them to a more close and constant dependence for their support upon Himself, and to make them more watchful against all future occasions of sin, and for sundry other just and holy ends (2 Cor. 12:7–9; Ps. 73; 77:1, 10, 12; Mark 14:66f.; John 21:15–17).

As God orders His world, His plan includes seasons when His own children are given over to various temptations and corruptions. Not only does He do this, but He does it often. The reason He does this is to chastise us for previous sin, or to teach us how bad we actually are. Without having our noses rubbed in it, we deceive ourselves on this point far too readily. God humbles us with our sins. When humbled, and aware of the deceitfulness of our own hearts, we are far more dependent upon Him, and far more wary than we would have been otherwise. In short, God works many wonderful things into the lives of His people through His practice of making us eat our own cooking.

6. As for those wicked and ungodly men whom God, as a righteous Judge, for former sins, doth blind and harden (Rom. 1:24, 26, 28; 11:7–8), from them He not only withholdeth His grace whereby they might have been enlightened in their understandings, and wrought upon in their hearts (Deut. 29:4); but sometimes also withdraweth the gifts which they had (Matt. 13:12; 25:29), and exposes them to such objects as their corruption makes occasion of sin (Deut. 2:30; 2 Ki. 8:12–13); and, withal, gives them over to their own lusts, the temptations of the world, and the power of Satan (Ps. 81:11–12; 2 Thess. 2:10–12), whereby it comes to pass that they harden themselves, even under those means which God useth for the softening of others (Exod. 7:3; 8:15, 32; 2 Cor. 2:15–16; Isa. 8:14; 1 Pet. 2:7–8; Isa. 6:9–10; Acts 28:26–27).

But God uses sin, not just as a wise Physician, but also as an indignant Judge and Executioner. Other men, no better or worse in themselves than the elect, are blinded and hardened because of their previous sins. Grace is withheld from them, but we must remember that grace is a gift, *not a wage.* If that withheld grace had been given, then their understanding would have come into light, and a gracious work would have been done in their hearts. But God not only withholds grace, He sometimes also removes what gifts they had in the first place and lets them run headlong. When His wrath is manifested, He gives free rein to their lusts, the lies of the world, and the power of the devil. When God lets go of a man and the man runs headlong, this is the wrath of God. The result of all this is a continuing hardening, even when the same external means (used in the salvation of others) is being used.

> 7. As the providence of God doth, in general, reach to all creatures; so, after a most special manner, it taketh care of His Church, and disposeth all things to the good thereof (1 Tim. 4:10; Amos 9:8–9; Rom. 8:28; Isa. 43:3–5, 14).

God's providence is in everything. But in the affairs of the Church, it is in everything for good. The Church is at the center of God's plan and purpose for this creation, and since the world is governed according to God's most wise counsel, we are not to approach trial and turmoil as Stoics. The world is not God's monkey house, despite the appearances sometimes. This means that God's saints must look, by faith, for that good which God says He is working.

CHAPTER 6
Of the Fall of Man, of Sin,
and of the Punishment Thereof

We must also remember our moral condition in this world governed by God, and where this moral condition came from.

> 1. Our first parents, being seduced by the subtilty and temptation of Satan, sinned, in eating the forbidden fruit (Gen. 3:13; 2 Cor. 11:3). This their sin, God was pleased, according to His wise and holy counsel, to permit, having purposed to order it to His own glory (Rom. 11:32).

Although Genesis does not mention Satan by name in the account of the temptation in the Garden, the Confession is right to place him there. The devil, the apostle John tells us, was sinning from the beginning, and was involved in the murder of Abel (1 Jn. 3: 8, 12). He also says in the Revelation that the devil was "that ancient serpent" (Rev. 12:9), and is called a dragon in that place. Placing the biblical data together, including Num. 21:9, we may conjecture that the devil had been of the seraphim, a heavenly winged serpent, a great dragon.

He seduced our first parents into eating the forbidden fruit, which corresponded to the lust of the flesh, the lust of the eyes, and the pride of life. It was good to eat, pleasant to look on, and would make one wise. God permitted this to happen, having a more glorious result and end in mind than would have been achieved had He prevented the sin. That glorious end was to be His own glory. Two of the most glorious attributes of God—justice and mercy—would have gone unrevealed in a world without sin.

> 2. By this sin they fell from their original righteousness and communion, with God (Gen. 3:6–8; Eccl. 7:29; Rom. 3:23), and so became dead in sin (Gen. 2:17; Eph. 2:1), and wholly defiled in all the parts and faculties of soul and body (Titus 1:15; Gen. 6:5; Jer. 17:9; Rom. 3:10–18).

Because of this sin, Adam and Eve fell from their original state of righteousness and fellowship with God. The end result of their sin was just what God had promised—the day you eat of the fruit of the tree in the middle of the Garden you shall surely die—and so the human race came to live in death. Some Christians call this state "total depravity," but this is misleading, making it sound like "absolute depravity." But the meaning of this doctrine is not that men are infinitely wicked, but rather that men are actually dead. We consequently have total inability with regard to saving ourselves, or preparing ourselves to be saved. Every aspect of man is fallen, wholly defiled in "all the parts and faculties" of the soul and body. In other words, there is no place within a man where that man could "stand" in order to get a grip on himself, to pull himself out of sin. The phrase "wholly defiled in all" captures the sense of this doctrine, like a thimble of ink stirred into a glass of water—the ink can get into everything without it becoming a glass of ink.

> 3. They being the root of all mankind, the guilt of this sin was imputed (Gen. 1:27–28; 2:16–17; Acts 17:26; Rom. 5:12, 15–19; 1 Cor. 15:21–22, 45, 49); and the same death in sin, and corrupted

nature, conveyed to all their posterity descending from them by ordinary generation (Ps. 51:5; Gen. 5:3; Job 14:4; 15:14).

The first Adam bestows the same kind of things which the second Adam does—here we see what falls in those categories corresponding to justification and sanctification. The guilt of Adam's sin was reckoned to the entire race. In other words, we have had the unrighteousness of his disobedience imputed to us. At the same time, we have also inherited (in a most practical way) the fact of death, and the corruption of our nature. This is passed on to everyone who is descended from Adam and Eve.

> 4. From this original corruption, whereby we are utterly indisposed, disabled, and made opposite to all good (Rom. 5:6; 8:7; 7:18; Col 1:21), and wholly inclined to all evil (Gen. 6:5; 8:21; Rom. 3:10–12), do proceed all actual transgressions (James 1:14–15; Eph. 2:2–3; Matt. 15:19).

From the nature of the tree proceeds the nature of the fruit. Because we have inherited this corruption of nature from Adam, our actions are naturally corrupt. Taking this in natural order, the first problem is what we are in Adam, the second problem is what I am because of Adam, and the third problem is what I do.

> 5. This corruption of nature, during this life, doth remain in those that are regenerated (1 John 1:8, 10; Rom. 7:14, 17–18, 23; James 3:2; Prov. 20:9; Eccl. 7:20); and although it be, through Christ, pardoned, and mortified; yet both itself, and all the motions thereof, are truly and properly sin (Rom. 7:5, 7–8, 25; Gal. 5:17).

The reason Christians continue to struggle with sin within themselves is because this corruption of nature remains even in those who are converted. Our prior condition was one of *reigning* sin. The condition of believers now is that of subdued (albeit *remaining*) sin. By nature, the believer still retains his Adamic corruptions. However, because of the new creation in Christ, those sins and inclinations are both pardoned and mortified. However, they remain in and with us, and they remain sin. The false ideal of sinless perfection in this life is consequently a lie. Those who believe in sinless perfection in this life should practice what they profess, and that would require abandoning this lie.

> 6. Every sin, both original and actual, being a transgression of the righteous law of God, and contrary thereunto (1 John 3:4), doth, in its own nature, bring guilt upon the sinner (Rom. 2:15; 3:9, 19), whereby he is bound over to the wrath of God (Eph. 2:3), and curse of the law (Gal. 3:10), and so made subject to death (Rom. 6:23), with all miseries spiritual (Eph. 4:18), temporal (Rom. 8:20; Lam. 3:39), and eternal (Matt. 25:41; 2 Thess. 1:9).

We are condemned and guilty not only for what we do, but also for what we are. The sin imputed to us is ours, and the sin we commit is ours. Sin is defined by the law of God, and not by what our nature enables us to perform or avoid. Because we are thus constituted sinners, we are under the wrath of God and the curse of the law. The result of this for us is death and all misery. The miseries which come upon us are spiritual, temporal and eternal.

Unit Four: For Further Study

 Reading Assignments

Hodge, pp. 80–104 [Chapters 4–5]

Vincent, pp. 44–54 [Questions 8–12]

Turretin, Vol. 1, pp. 494–501[Sixth Topic: Questions 2–3]

 Questions on Reading

1. What was the nature of the God who created the elements of the world out of nothing?

2. What does Hodge mean by "absolute making"?

3. What is meant by *creatio prima* and *creatio secunda*?

4. According to Vincent, what does the image of God not consist of?

5. What does it consist of?

6. How does Vincent define a covenant?

7. In what way does Turretin respond to the charge of fatalism?

8. What does he mean by "Christian fate"?

9. How many things are under the providence of God?

10. Are free and voluntary actions governed by providence?

UNIT FIVE

CHAPTER 7
Of God's Covenant With Man

We now come to consider how God deals with man, which is always through a covenant.

> 1. The distance between God and the creature is so great, that although reasonable creatures do owe obedience unto Him as their Creator, yet they could never have any fruition of Him as their blessedness and reward, but by some voluntary condescension on God's part, which He hath been pleased to express by way of covenant (Isa. 40:13–17; Job 9:32–33; 1 Sam. 2:25; Ps. 113:5–6; 100:2–3; Job 22:2–3; 35:7–8; Luke 17:10; Acts 17:24–25).

We must always recall the Creator/creature divide, a divide which exists in the very nature of things quite apart from the issue of sin. Our sinfulness is one thing, and our finitude another, and the two things must not be confounded or confused. It is not a sin to be a creature. At the same time, there are ramifications to being a creature. The first is a natural and necessary duty to render obedience to God. At the same time, no *external* necessity requires that God stoop to bless us through His presence, other than the necessity resulting from the graciousness of God's character. When God condescends to commune with us as creatures, He does so by way of covenant.

When everything is considered together, we see that the very fabric of the created order is covenantal.

> 2. The first covenant made with man was a covenant of works (Gal. 3:12), wherein life was promised to Adam; and in him to his posterity (Rom. 10:5; 5:12–20), upon condition of perfect and personal obedience (Gen. 2:17; Gal. 3:10).

Periodically, great Homer nods, and I believe that is the case here. While there is no necessary problem with the *doctrine*, the Westminster divines have (I believe) named this covenant poorly. To call this covenant with Adam a covenant "of works" leads people to confuse it either with the Old Testament economy, or with pharisaical distortions of the law. This misunderstanding is evident in the scriptural reference given for this point. To call it works opposes it, in the scriptural terminology, to grace. But the covenant given to Adam prior to the Fall was in no way opposed to grace. It would be far better to call this pre-Fall covenant *a covenant of creation*, or the *covenant of life*, which it is called elsewhere in the Westminster Standards. In this covenant, life was promised to Adam and his descendents as the fruit of perfect and personal obedience. But notice the word *fruit*—as a covenant of creation, grace is not opposed to it, and grace permeates the whole. If by "covenant of works" we mean raw merit, then we have to deny the covenant of works. But if this covenant made with Adam was inherently gracious (as many Reformed theologians have held), then the only problem is the choice of words. And, with regard to whether the covenant was gracious, a simple thought experiment will suffice. If Adam had withstood temptation successfully, would he have had any obligation to say "thank You" to God? If not, then it is not a gracious covenant. If so, then it was.

3. Man, by his fall, having made himself incapable of life by that covenant, the Lord was pleased to make a second (Gal. 3:21; Rom. 8:3; 3:20–21; Gen. 3:15; Isa. 42:6), commonly called the covenant of grace; wherein He freely offereth unto sinners life and salvation by Jesus Christ; requiring of them faith in Him, that they may be saved (Mark 16:15, 16; John 3:16; Rom. 10:6, 9; Gal. 3:11), and promising to give unto all those that are ordained unto eternal life His Holy Spirit, to make them willing, and able to believe (Ezek. 36:26–27; John 6:44–45).

Since the first covenant was broken, another covenant was necessary if things were to be repaired. It is also necessary not to confuse this first covenant with the Old Covenant and the second covenant with the New Covenant. The first covenant under discussion is the ante-lapsarian covenant; the second covenant spans all human history after the Fall. In this second covenant, a covenant of grace, God offers salvation and life to sinners through Jesus Christ. As the message of this covenant comes to a sinner, God promises salvation through faith. In this covenant, God also commits to grant His Holy Spirit to all those ordained to eternal life. When this gift is bestowed, the Spirit makes the sinner willing and able to believe. When he believes, God hears his cry for salvation. God requires faith of the sinner, and gives what He requires.

4. This covenant of grace is frequently set forth in Scripture by the name of a testament, in reference to the death of Jesus Christ the Testator, and to the everlasting inheritance, with all things belonging to it, therein bequeathed (Heb. 9:15, 16–17; 7:22; Luke 22:20; 1 Cor. 11:25).

This covenant of grace is described in Scripture as a *testament*. As a testament, we find ourselves more than just parties to a covenant. We are also set forth as heirs. The fruit of the covenant is directly related to the death of the Testator.

5. This covenant was differently administered in the time of the law, and in the time of the gospel (2 Cor. 3:6–9): under the law it was administered by promises, prophecies, sacrifices, circumcision, the paschal lamb, and other types and ordinances delivered to the people of the Jews, all foresignifying Christ to come (Heb. 8, 9, 10; Rom. 4:11; Col. 2:11–12; 1 Cor. 5:7); which were, for that time, sufficient and efficacious, through the operation of the Spirit, to instruct and build up the elect in faith in the promised Messiah (1 Cor. 10:1–4; Heb. 11:13; John 8:56), by whom they had full remission of sins, and eternal salvation; and is called the old Testament (Gal. 3:7–9, 14).

This covenant of grace has undergone differing administrations. In the time of the law, the covenant of grace was administered with a view to the future. The saints of the Old Testament looked forward in faith to the fruition of all the promises, prophecies, etc. Everything in the Old Testament looks forward. By the grace of God, the gospel presented in this fashion was "sufficient and efficacious" through the Spirit to establish the elect of God. The elect in the time of the law had full forgiveness of sin, and were partakers of the gift of eternal life. The covenant of grace under this administration is called the Old Testament. It is important to emphasize that according to the Westminster Confession, the Mosaic economy was an administration of the covenant of *grace*, not an administration of the covenant of works. The language is very plain here: the covenant of grace was administered one way under the law and another way in the time of the gospel. Those who want a recapitulation of the covenant of works within the Mosaic economy are either running the grave risk of blurring the two covenants, which is genuinely problematic, or they are denying the teaching of the Confession here and saying that the Mosaic economy was a covenant of works, which is dangerous.

6. Under the gospel, when Christ, the substance (Col. 2:17), was exhibited, the ordinances in which this covenant is dispensed are the preaching of the Word, and the administration of the sacraments of Baptism and the Lord's Supper (Matt. 28:19–20; 1 Cor. 11:23–25): which, though fewer in number, and administered with more simplicity, and less outward glory, yet, in them, it is held forth in more fullness, evidence, and spiritual efficacy (Heb. 12:22–27; Jer. 31:33–34), to all nations, both Jews and Gentiles (Matt. 28:19; Eph. 2:15–19); and is called the new Testament (Luke 22:20). There are not therefore two covenants of grace, differing in substance, but one and the same, under various dispensations (Gal. 3:14, 16; Acts 15:11; Rom. 3:21–23, 30. Ps. 32:1; Rom. 4:3, 6, 16–17, 23–24; Heb. 13:8).

Under the time of the gospel, this one covenant of grace receives a different and simpler administration. The substance of the covenant has come, the Lord Jesus Christ, and the ordinances and sacraments are therefore altered—necessarily so. The ordinances of this administration are the preaching of the Word and the administration of the two sacraments. Notice that the covenant is "dispensed" through the preaching of the Word and the administration of the sacraments. The sacraments here are not called reminders, but rather dispensers.

The things we are called upon to do in this administration are simpler, and have less "less outward glory." But in the gospel economy, the last are first, and this diminution of glory results in greater glory. In the simplicity of Christian worship, the gospel comes in power to all nations, both Jew and Gentile. This manner of worship is called the New Testament.

The division between the covenants, therefore, does not come between Malachi and Matthew. The two testaments simply describe one and the same covenant of grace. The sin of pharisaism is not a separate covenant made for blessing by God at all, but rather a distortion of the covenant of grace as it was given in the time of the law. God never commanded men to save themselves. Salvation has always been by grace alone through faith alone.

CHAPTER 8
Of Christ the Mediator

With lost and sinful men, a covenant must have a mediator.

1. It pleased God, in His eternal purpose, to choose and ordain the Lord Jesus, His only begotten Son, to be the Mediator between God and man (Isa. 42:1; 1 Pet. 1:19–20; John 3:16; 1 Tim. 2:5), the Prophet (Acts 3:22), Priest (Heb. 5:5–6), and King (Ps. 2:6. Luke 1:33), the Head and Savior of His Church (Eph. 5:23), the Heir of all things (Heb. 1:2), and Judge of the world (Acts 17:31): unto whom He did from all eternity give a people, to be His seed (John 17:6; Ps. 22:30; Isa. 53:10), and to be by Him in time redeemed, called, justified, sanctified, and glorified (1 Tim. 2:6; Isa. 55:4–5; 1 Cor. 1:30).

Jesus Christ is the Elect of God. This election is not the same as the eternal begetting of the Son by the Father, but is rather a sovereign appointment to the position of a Mediator. The appointment presupposes a human race in need of a Mediator. The basis of this ordination is the good pleasure of God.

The only-begotten was chosen to fill many offices. The first was that of Mediator, bridging the divide between men and God. He was ordained to teach His people, filling the office of Prophet. He was chosen to be our Priest, presenting a sacrifice on our behalf to God. He was chosen to be King, so that we might have someone to rule over us. His position of authority is organic: He is the Head and Savior of the Church. He will inherit everything and will be the sovereign judge over all things. From all eternity, a particular people were given to the Son to be His seed, and what we call history is actually the process in which we see the outworking of that gift. In history, we were redeemed, called, justified, sanctified, and glorified.

> 2. The Son of God, the second person of the Trinity, being very and eternal God, of one substance and equal with the Father, did, when the fullness of time was come, take upon Him man's nature (John 1:1, 14; 1 John 5:20; Phil. 2:6; Gal. 4:4), with all the essential properties, and common infirmities thereof, yet without sin (Heb. 2:14, 16–17; Heb. 4:15); being conceived by the power of the Holy Ghost, in the womb of the virgin Mary, of her substance (Luke 1:27, 31, 35; Gal. 4:4). So that two whole, perfect, and distinct natures, the Godhead and the manhood, were inseparably joined together in one person, without conversion, composition, or confusion (Luke 1:35; Col. 2:9; Rom 9:5; 1 Pet. 3:18; 1 Tim. 3:16). Which person is very God, and very man, yet one Christ, the only Mediator between God and man (Rom. 1:3–4; 1 Tim. 2:5).

The second person of the Trinity, being infinite, added the finitude of human nature to His attributes. The finitude of the human nature of Christ is not to be understood as a subtraction from the divine nature. In taking on human nature, He took on all its essential properties and limitations, the only exception being sin. The fact that He was conceived by the Holy Ghost did not make Mary a "surrogate mother." He was conceived without a human father, but was conceived "of her substance." In other words, she was His mother in every sense of the word.

The two natures were inseparably joined in this hypostatic union, which is to say, the Incarnation was permanent. Neither of the natures was altered by this union, meaning that the one person involved, the Lord Jesus Christ, is truly God and truly man. If we conceive of this union in a way that makes sturdy common sense to us, then that means we have fallen into heresy. This is the miracle of miracles.

> 3. The Lord Jesus, in His human nature thus united to the divine, was sanctified, and anointed with the Holy Spirit, above measure (Ps. 45:7; John 3:34), having in Him all the treasures of wisdom and knowledge (Col. 2:3); in whom it pleased the Father that all fullness should dwell (Col. 1:19); to the end that, being holy, harmless, undefiled, and full of grace and truth (Heb. 7:26; John 1:14), He might be thoroughly furnished to execute the office of a Mediator and Surety (Acts 10:38; Heb. 12:28; 7:22). Which office He took not unto Himself, but was thereunto called by His Father (Heb. 5:4–5), who put all power and judgment into His hand, and gave Him commandment to execute the same (John 5:22, 27; Matt. 28:18; Acts 2:36).

The human nature of Christ did not "tag along" as He fulfilled the ministry appointed to Him. The Spirit of God was upon Him, sanctifying and anointing Him as man above all measure. Because of the work of the Spirit, Christ was filled with all wisdom and knowledge, and in Him all fullness came to dwell. The human nature of Christ was not a hindrance in the work of mediation, but was rather an essential aspect of His qualification to execute that office.

He did not push Himself into that office, but was called to it by His Father. The Father entrusted Him to render all judgment and commanded Him to fill His office.

The expressions of Scripture which describe Him as growing, obeying, being filled, resisting temptation, etc. are all to be understood of Christ in His humanity.

4. This office the Lord Jesus did most willingly undertake (Ps. 40:7–8; Heb. 10:5–10; John 10:18; Phil. 2:8); which that He might discharge, He was made under the law (Gal. 4:4), and did perfectly fulfill it (Matt. 3:15; 5:17); endured most grievous torments immediately in His soul (Matt. 26:37–38; Luke 22:44; Matt. 27:46), and most painful sufferings in His body (Matt. 26; 27); was crucified, and died (Phil 2:8), was buried, and remained under the power of death, yet saw no corruption (Acts 2:23–24, 27; 13:37; Rom 6:9). On the third day He arose from the dead (1 Cor. 15:3–5), with the same body in which He suffered (John 20:25, 27), with which also He ascended into heaven, and there sitteth at the right hand of His Father (Mark 16:19), making intercession (Rom. 8:34; Heb. 9:24; 7:25), and shall return, to judge men and angels, at the end of the world (Rom. 14:9–10; Acts 1:11; 10:42; Matt. 13:40–42; Jude 6; 2 Pet. 2:4).

Christ willingly submitted to this requirement of the Father. In order to enable Him to perform His ministry, He was born of a woman, under the law. He lived in obedience to the law perfectly. Despite His obedience (and in some senses *because* of it), He suffered grievously. He was crucified, He died, and was buried briefly. He was not in the grave long enough to see corruption. When He rose from the dead, it was with and in the same body He had during His passion. He has that same body now that He has ascended into Heaven, where He has a position of ultimate authority at the Father's right hand. In Heaven, He prays for His saints, and will return from Heaven to judge all men and angels, which He will do at the end of the world.

5. The Lord Jesus, by His perfect obedience, and sacrifice of Himself, which He through the eternal Spirit, once offered up unto God, has fully satisfied the justice of His Father (Rom 5:19; Heb. 9:14, 16; 10:14; Eph 5:2; Rom. 3:25–26); and purchased, not only

reconciliation, but an everlasting inheritance in the kingdom of heaven, for all those whom the Father has given unto Him (Dan. 9:24, 26; Col. 1:19–20; Eph. 1:11, 14; John 17:2; Heb. 9:12, 15).

The Confession here does not make a point of distinguishing between the active and passive obedience of Christ. According to this division, there were two aspects to the obedience of Christ. The first was the active perfect obedience of His sinless life. The second was the "passive" obedience rendered when He submitted Himself to the ignominy of death on the cross. Through the Spirit, His entire obedience was offered to the Father and satisfied the justice of God the Father. This offering purchased more than simple forgiveness and reconciliation—He secured by this offering an everlasting inheritance to be enjoyed by all the saints given to Him by the Father. While the point of this division is an important one, we need to recognize that it is the righteousness of Christ's entire obedience that is imputed to us, and not the righteousness of Christ on even-numbered days along with the righteousness of Christ on odd-numbered days. If theological divisions help us understand that we have all of Christ, then well and good. If not, we should perhaps not overanalyze it.

> 6. Although the work of redemption was not actually wrought by Christ till after His incarnation, yet the virtue, efficacy, and benefits thereof were communicated unto the elect, in all ages successively from the beginning of the world, in and by those promises, types, and sacrifices, wherein He was revealed, and signified to be the seed of the woman which should bruise the serpent's head; and the Lamb slain from the beginning of the world; being yesterday and to–day the same, and forever (Gal. 4:4–5; Gen. 3:15; Rev. 13:8; Heb. 13:8).

Every saint in the history of the world has been saved in the same way, by the same gospel. The saints who lived before the Incarnation were saved by looking in faith at the promises of God, including the gospel preached in the types and sacrifices. The entire Old Testament points to the coming Christ, and believers were those who believed that God would fulfill His word. God, for His part, knew what He was going to do, with no possibility of anything else being done, and so He could apply the virtues, efficacy, and benefits of Christ's death to these forward-looking saints. But of course, this would not have been possible unless God had predestined the obedience of Christ.

> 7. Christ, in the work of mediation, acts according to both natures, by each nature doing that which is proper to itself (Heb. 9:14; 1 Pet. 3:18); yet, by reason of the unity of the person, that which is proper to one nature is sometimes in Scripture attributed to the person denominated by the other nature (Acts 20:28; John 3:13; 1 John 3:16).

This is simply the teaching of the Definition of Chalcedon. What is predicated of one nature may be predicated of the person, but not of the other nature properly. But in the common way of speaking, a man might say, "Christ, the divine Son of God, resisted temptation." It is proper to speak this way, but only if we remember the nature of the divine and human "categories."

> 8. To all those for whom Christ has purchased redemption, He does certainly and effectually apply and communicate the same (John 6:37, 39; 10:15–16); making intercession for them (1 John 2:1–2; Rom. 8:34), and revealing unto them, in and by the Word, the mysteries of salvation (John 15:13, 15; Eph. 1:7–9; John 17:6); effectually persuading them by His Spirit to believe and obey, and governing their hearts by His Word and Spirit (John 14:16; Heb. 12:2; 2 Cor. 4:13; Rom. 8:9, 14; 15:18–19; John 17:17); overcoming all their enemies by His almighty power and wisdom, in such manner, and ways, as are most consonant to His wonderful and unsearchable dispensation (Ps. 110:1; 1 Cor. 15:25–26; Mal. 4:2–3; Col. 2:15).

Once Christ has purchased redemption for His elect, He is not done with them. He also applies this redemption to them, He prays for them to the Father, He teaches them the way of salvation, He sends His Spirit to persuade them of the gospel, which brings them to faith and obedience, He becomes the ruler of their hearts by means of His Word and Spirit, and He conquers all their enemies—in such a fashion as seems good to Him.

Unit Five: For Further Study

 Reading Assignments

Hodge, pp. 105–119 [Chapter 6]

Vincent, pp. 54–67 [Questions 13–19]

 Questions on Reading

1. According to Hodge, in what moral state were our first parents created?

2. Since Adam could be tested and could fail, what sort of state was that?

3. When our first parents sinned, what happened to them?

4. In what two ways was Adam the head of all mankind?

5. What happens in true conviction of sin?

6. What is meant by freedom of the will, according to Vincent?

7. Where does Vincent say the law of God is to be found?

8. Why did God forbid the tree of knowledge of good and evil?

9. Why was the Lord Jesus not entailed in the fall of Adam?

10. In what two ways were we all in Adam when he sinned?

UNIT SIX

CHAPTER 9
Of Free Will

Now we come to the vexed problem of free will. Let us do what we can to vex it some more.

> 1. God hath endued the will of man with that natural liberty, that it is neither forced, nor, by any absolute necessity of nature, determined to good, or evil (Matt. 17:12; James 1:14; Deut. 30:19).

By virtue of creation, mankind was given a true and natural liberty with regard to all issues of good and evil. Adam, when he fell, was not coerced or dragged into that sin. The decree which God had given concerning the fall of man did not "force" Adam to his sin, and neither had God implanted within Adam any program of internal coercion. Now how can a non-coercive decree be a *sovereign* decree? The answer to *that* question resides in the fact that the "causal agent" in the sovereign decrees does not inhabit the same "universe" as the thing caused. If it did, then the causation on the one hand displaces responsibility on the other. In other words, God is to the universe what Shakespeare is to Macbeth, and not what Lady Macbeth is to Macbeth. Put another way, God's relation to the universe is *unlike every causal situation in the world that we know.* The fact that God determined how everything would go does not mean that He forced it the way we would have to force it to make something like this happen. But note that the Reformed position on the human will is that in the creation God gave it "natural liberty."

> 2. Man, in his state of innocency, had freedom, and power to will and to do that which was good and well pleasing to God (Eccl. 7:29; Gen. 1:26); but yet, mutably, so that he might fall from it (Gen. 2:16–17; 3:6).

Adam did not sin by any necessity related to how he had been created. He had the ability to do right. But this ability was no guarantee that he *would* do right—he was created with the capacity for sin.

> 3. Man, by his fall into a state of sin, hath wholly lost all ability of will to any spiritual good accompanying salvation (Rom. 5:6; 8:7; John 15:5): so as, a natural man, being altogether averse from that good (Rom. 3:10, 12), and dead in sin (Eph. 2:1, 5; Col. 2:13), is not able, by his own strength, to convert himself, or to prepare himself thereunto (John 6:44, 65; Eph. 2:2–5; 1 Cor. 2:14; Titus 3:13, 4–5).

We must begin our discussion of this important subject by distinguishing between physical liberty and moral liberty. Physical liberty means the ability to turn right or left, to raise one's hand or lower it, to choose chocolate or vanilla. Moral liberty means the ability to choose the right course of action, and to do so for the right reasons. Men as *creatures* have a physical liberty, but as *sinners* they have lost all moral liberty in Adam. The relation between physical liberty and the sovereignty of God presents an interesting philosophical problem, which should be addressed in accordance with the discussion above concerning paragraph one.

But the loss of moral liberty presents no problem whatever. The question there is not how to reconcile God's sovereignty in salvation with our moral liberty, *because we do not have any such liberty.* There is nothing there to reconcile; we do not assert liberty in this realm, and therefore do not have to explain how it can coexist with what God does. We are no more able to choose good for good reasons than a pig can choose to fly.

We consequently have no moral power, and this means we cannot convert ourselves, and we cannot prepare ourselves to be converted by God. In this regard, we do absolutely nothing. Man as creature is free—we have as much natural liberty to go right or left as Adam did. The Fall did not rob us of our creaturely liberty. The Fall did ensure the loss of our ability to choose what is right for the right reasons. In these respective realms of freedom, man as creature is free; man as sinner is not.

> 4. When God converts a sinner, and translates him into the state of grace, He freeth him from his natural bondage under sin (Col. 1:13; John 8:34, 36); and, by His grace alone, enables him freely to will and to do that which is spiritually good (Phil. 2:13; Rom 6:18, 22); yet so, as that by reason of his remaining corruption, he doth not perfectly, nor only, will that which is good, but doth also will that which is evil (Gal. 5:17; Rom. 7:15, 18–19, 21, 23).

After conversion, moral liberty is restored, but not completely and immutably restored. The restoration process begins. In other words, we are still capable of sin, and further, we are not capable of complete and final perfection. But the good we do is truly and genuinely good. Because it is not perfect, it cannot be considered as the ground of our justification before God, but it is nonetheless genuine.

> 5. The will of man is made perfectly and immutably free to do good alone in the state of glory only (Eph. 4:13; Heb. 12:23; 1 John 3:2; Jude 24).

True freedom is found in heaven, where we choose what is right and can do no other. Freedom is therefore not defined as the "power of contrary choice," but rather as the freedom to do nothing but right. By the former definition, God Himself is not free, and therefore is not a moral agent. If the "power of contrary choice" is essential to the identity of being a moral being, then God is not a moral being, and we will not be moral in heaven. This definition would make heaven nothing but an eternal moral prison. But the latter definition shows us where true freedom resides.

By way of summary, this is a good place to introduce Augustine's famous fourfold distinction:

1. Man's condition before the fall was *libertas Adami/posse non peccare*—the freedom of Adam/able not to sin.

2. Man's condition after the fall is *libertas peccatorum/non posse non peccare*—the (so-called) freedom of sinners/not able not to sin.

3. Man's condition in Christ is *libertas fidelium/posse peccare et non peccare*—the freedom of the faithful/able to sin and not sin.

4. And man's condition in the resurrection will be *libertas gloriae/non posse peccare*—the freedom of glory/not able to sin.

CHAPTER 10
Of Effectual Calling

How can we be set free from this condition of slavery?

1. All those whom God hath predestinated unto life, and those only, He is pleased, in His appointed and accepted time, effectually to call (Rom. 8:30, 11:7; Eph. 1:10–11), by His Word and Spirit (2 Thess. 2:13–14; 2 Cor. 3:3, 6), out of that state of sin and death, in which they are by nature to grace and salvation, by Jesus Christ (Rom. 8:2; Eph. 2:1–5; 2 Tim. 1:9–10); enlightening their minds spiritually and savingly to understand the things of God (Acts 26:18; 1 Cor. 2:10, 12; Eph. 1:17–18), taking away their heart of stone, and giving unto them an heart of flesh (Ezek. 36:26); renewing their wills, and, by His almighty power, determining them to that which is good (Ezek 11:19, 36:27; Phil. 2:13; Deut 30:6), and effectually drawing them to Jesus Christ (Eph. 1:19; John 6:44–45): yet so, as they come most freely, being made willing by His grace (Song 1:4; Ps. 110:3; John 6:37; Rom. 6:16–18).

All those and only those. The triune God does not work at variance with Himself in the work of salvation. Those predestinated unto life are the same who are called. They are called because God is pleased to do so and is pleased to do so when and how He has determined.

In other words, it is not just the salvation of Smith which pleases Him, but also the manner and time in which Smith comes. One constant is the fact that God calls by His Word and by His Spirit. Those saved are called out of their natural state of sin and death, and they are called into grace and salvation. Of course, all is done through Jesus Christ.

The result of this call is that their minds are enlightened so that they might understand the things of God. God takes away their stony heart and gives them a new heart. It is worth noting yet again that if a man could repent and believe with his old heart, he doesn't really need a new one. This bears repeating. What is the point of a new heart if all the essential evangelical duties (repentance and faith) can be performed with the old heart? God gives eyes, and afterwards we see. He does not give us new eyes as a reward for having seen with the old sightless eyes. God gives life and then we live. God renews and quickens their will, orients them to the good, and efficaciously draws them to Christ. But the fact that God draws them efficaciously does not mean that they are made into robots or puppets. They come most freely, genuinely wanting the salvation which God gave them the desire for.

This is not a true desire, some might say, if God gives it. But is desire for food true desire? Who gives that? Is desire for sex true desire? Who gives that? Thirty seconds of reflection should show that all our desires are given to us by God. We are creatures, after all.

> 2. This effectual call is of God's free and special grace alone, not from anything at all foreseen in man (2 Tim. 1:9; Titus 3:4–5; Eph. 2:4–5, 8–9; Rom. 9:11), who is altogether passive therein, until, being quickened and renewed by the Holy Spirit (1 Cor. 2:14; Rom. 8:7; Eph. 2:5), he is thereby enabled to answer this call, and to embrace the grace offered and conveyed in it (John 6:37; Ezek. 36:27; John 5:25).

No trickery may be used to get around the supremacy of God in this, and no intellectual time travel either. God does not look down the corridors of time, see people choosing Him, and then choose them as a consequence. God is no me-too-er. This effectual call is all of God, and man has no part in it—other than to benefit from the gift of it. Man is altogether passive until after the gift is given. Once the Holy Spirit quickens and renews him, he is then able to respond to the gift. Consequently, the order is effectual call, regeneration, repentance, faith in the gospel, and salvation. The order is "Jesus speaks, and then Lazarus comes out of the grave."

> 3. Elect infants, dying in infancy, are regenerated, and saved by Christ, through the Spirit (Luke 18:15–16; Acts 2:38–39; John 3:3, 5; 1 John 5:12; Rom. 8:9), who worketh when, and where, and how He pleaseth (John 3:8): so also are all other elect persons who are incapable of being outwardly called by the ministry of the Word (1 John 5:12; Acts 4:12).

With a great deal of practical wisdom, the Confession says nothing about the state of infants who die as infants, other than to say that some of the elect are found among them. Where the Bible is silent, so should we be. Such infants (and others, like those severely retarded) are regenerated and saved by Christ, through the Spirit, even though we cannot see how the outward ministry of the Word relates. In this, as with all things, God remains King and Sovereign.

> 4. Others, not elected, although they may be called by the ministry of the Word (Matt. 22:14), and may have some common operations of the Spirit (Matt. 7:22; 13:20–21; Heb. 6:4–5), yet they never truly come unto Christ, and therefore cannot be saved (John 6:64–66; 8:24): much less can men, not professing the Christian religion, be saved in any other way whatsoever, be they never so diligent to frame their lives according to the light of nature, and

the laws of that religion they do profess (Acts 4:12; John 14:6; Eph. 2:12; John 4:22; 17:3). And to assert and maintain that they may, is very pernicious, and to be detested (2 John 9–11; 1 Cor. 16:22; Gal. 1:6–8).

The non-elect who hear the ministry of the Word cannot patch together their own salvation from those things which they hear and experience. They may even experience some common operations of the Spirit, and yet still not be saved. If this is the case, still less can someone patch together a code of conduct from the light of nature and whatever Tao they may happen to possess. Their diligence in patching this together will be revealed in the last day as no diligence at all. To surmise that men can be saved apart from the declaration of the gospel is, our fathers tell us, a mischievous error, and a detestable one.

Unit Six: For Further Study

 Reading Assignments

Hodge, pp. 159–178 [Chapters 9–10]

Vincent, pp. 214–219, 89–92 [Questions 82, 29–32]

Turretin, Vol. 1, pp. 659–683 [Tenth Topic: Questions 1–4] and Vol. 2, 504–510, 546–558; Fifteenth Topic: Questions 2, 6]

Questions on Reading

1. How does Hodge describe man's faculty of self-determination?

2. What can an act of will from an unregenerate man not do?

3. What two kinds of call are distinguished by Hodge?

4. According to Vincent, was man ever able to keep the command of God perfectly?

5. How often do God's saints break the commandments of God?

6. What is an ineffectual calling?

7. Does Turretin object to the use of the phrase *free will*?

8. Are necessity and free will ever inconsistent?

9. Are the reprobate called by God?

10. Why does God offer salvation to the reprobate?

UNIT SEVEN

CHAPTER 11
Of Justification

Justification is the article of a standing or falling church, as Luther once put it. It is crucial for us to get it right.

> 1. Those whom God effectually calls, He also freely justifieth (Rom. 8:30; 3:24); not by infusing righteousness into them, but by pardoning their sins, and by accounting and accepting their persons as righteous; not for any thing wrought in them, or done by them, but for Christ's sake alone; nor by imputing faith itself, the act of believing, or any other evangelical obedience to them, as their righteousness; but by imputing the obedience and satisfaction of Christ unto them (Rom. 4:5–8; 2 Cor. 5:19, 21; Rom. 3:22, 24–25, 27–28; Titus 3:5, 7; Eph. 1:7; Jer. 23:6; 1 Cor. 1:30–31; Rom. 5:17–19), they receiving and resting on Him and His righteousness by faith; which faith they have not of themselves, it is the gift of God (Acts 10:44; Gal. 2:16; Phil. 3:9; Acts 13:38–39; Eph. 2:7–8).

God justifies those whom He effectually calls, but this justification must not be understood as an *infusion* of righteousness. Rather, justification is the pardon for sins, and the legal reckoning of our persons as righteous. It is important that we do not stumble through a misunderstanding of the basis of this. We are justified for Christ's sake only. God does not justify us for anything done *by* us, and, far more important, for anything done *in* us (even by Him). Nor does God justify us because of our faith—rather He justifies us because of Christ's obedience and work, and this is appropriated by us through faith. There is a crucial difference between "through faith" and "on account of faith." Understanding these prepositions (in the gut, not in the head) is a matter of life and death, heaven and hell.

Imputation is a forensic and declaratory action. It is frequently seen in the courtroom, as when a defendant is declared "not guilty." When that declaration is made, imputation rays do not fly across the courtroom and create non-guiltiness in the defendant. Rather it is *a declaration of status*. But a courtroom is not the only place where this kind of forensic declaration occurs. "I now pronounce you husband and wife" is another example of this. At that moment, all that he has becomes hers. All that is hers becomes his.

> 2. Faith, thus receiving and resting on Christ and His righteousness, is the alone instrument of justification (John 1:12; Rom. 3:28; 5:1): yet is it not alone in the person justified, but is ever accompanied with all other saving graces, and is no dead faith, but worketh by love (James 2:17, 22, 26; Gal. 5:6).

We are saved through faith alone, but never through a faith that is alone. Saving faith is never lonely faith. We can separate faith from other graces and virtues logically and conceptually, but not practically. We may distinguish, but never separate.

It is the "alone instrument" in the hands of God as He effects the justification of a sinner. The Confession explicitly states, however, that faith is not alone in the life of the one justified. Justifying faith, in the heart of the one justified, is always and necessarily accompanied by all the other saving graces.

Not only is justifying faith closely accompanied by other saving graces, we are also taught something here about the quality of this justifying faith. It is a living faith—"no dead faith"—and it works by love. The way that justifying faith expresses its life, making its presence known, is by working in love. Since love is the subject of the greatest two commandments, justifying faith expresses its life through living obedience, and never through dead works.

> 3. Christ, by His obedience and death, did fully discharge the debt of all those that are thus justified, and did make a proper, real, and full satisfaction to His Father's justice in their behalf (Rom 5:8–10, 19; 1 Tim. 2:5–6; Heb. 10:10, 14; Dan. 9:24, 26; Isa. 53:4–6, 10–12). Yet, in as much as He was given by the Father for them (Rom. 8:32); and His obedience and satisfaction accepted in their stead (2 Cor. 5:21; Matt. 3:17; Eph. 5:2); and both, freely, not for any thing in them; their justification is only of free grace (Rom. 3:24; Eph. 1:7); that both the exact justice, and rich grace of God might be glorified in the justification of sinners (Rom. 3:26; Eph. 2:7).

Pardon for sins is a great part of our justification. The debt for our sins was paid for through Christ's obedience and death. On our behalf Christ genuinely satisfied the justice of the Father. Our justification reveals two aspects of God's nature and character—His justice displayed in Christ and His mercy displayed in Christ. In this great transaction, our sins were imputed to Christ, and His righteousness imputed to us. The former reveals God's justice, and the latter His mercy.

> 4. God did, from all eternity, decree to justify all the elect (Gal. 3:8; 1 Pet. 1:2, 19–20; Rom. 8:30), and Christ did, in the fullness of time, die for their sins, and rise again for their justification (Gal. 4:4; 1 Tim. 2:6; Rom. 4:25): nevertheless, they are not justified, until the Holy Spirit doth, in due time, actually apply Christ unto them (Col. 1:21–22; Gal. 2:16; Titus 3:4–7).

The decision to justify and the laying of the foundation for justifying are not the same as justifying. God made the decision to justify His elect before the world was created. The ground of justification was established two thousand years ago. But the actual justification does not occur until the individual concerned actually receives pardon for sins.

> 5. God doth continue to forgive the sins of those that are justified (Matt. 6:12; 1 John 1:7, 9; 2:1–2); and, although they can never fall from the state of justification (Luke 22:32; John 10:28; Heb. 10:14), yet they may, by their sins, fall under God's fatherly displeasure, and not have the light of His countenance restored unto them, until they humble themselves, confess their sins, beg pardon, and renew their faith and repentance (Ps 89:31–33; 51:7–12; 32:5; Matt. 26:75; 1 Cor. 11:30, 32; Luke 1:20).

Justification is permanent, and God never ceases to see a justified person as perfect. That status is unalterable. This has reference to the person's legal status; they are secure in their position within the family of God. And yet, precisely because they are in the family of God, God does exhibit a fatherly displeasure for sin. It is the difference between having justification and having the joy of justification. A child awaiting a spanking in the basement is just as much a member of the family as he ever was. However, it can safely be said that he is not happy about being a member of the family. His membership is perhaps the current ground of his discontent.

> 6. The justification of believers under the old testament was, in all these respects, one and the same with the justification of believers under the new testament (Gal. 3:9, 13–14; Rom. 4:22–24; Heb. 13:8).

We cannot make a distinction between the saints of the Old Testament and the saints of the New in this respect. They may and do differ with regard to gifts and graces, but justification is the *sine qua non* of being a saint of God.

CHAPTER 12
Of Adoption

Adoption is where many of our gospel privileges find a place of rest.

1. All those that are justified, God vouchsafeth, in and for His only Son Jesus Christ, to make partakers of the grace of adoption (Eph. 1:5; Gal. 4:4–5), by which they are taken into the number, and enjoy the liberties and privileges of the children of God (Rom. 8:17; John 1:12), have His name put upon them (Jer. 14:9; 2 Cor. 6:18; Rev. 3:12), receive the spirit of adoption (Rom. 8:15), have access to the throne of grace with boldness (Eph. 3:12; Rom. 5:2), are enabled to cry, Abba, Father (Gal. 4:6), are pitied (Ps. 103:13), protected (Prov. 14:26), provided for (Matt. 6:30, 32; 1 Pet. 5:7), and chastened by Him as by a Father (Heb. 12:6): yet never cast off (Lam. 3:31), but sealed to the day of redemption (Eph. 4:30); and inherit the promises (Heb. 6:12), as heirs of everlasting salvation (1 Pet. 1:3–4; Heb. 1:14).

As a consequence of justification, God promises to bring those justified into His family as adopted children. This inclusion is itself a grace, the grace of adoption, and it has many attendant privileges. The first is that we take on the name of the family; we are Christians. Not only are we adopted, we receive the spirit of adoption. Because we now belong to the household, we can walk right in. Our relationship to the Father is such that we may cry out to Him as *Abba*. He, in His capacity as Father, pities us, protects us, supplies our needs, and spanks us. The relationship cannot be undone, as we are sealed for the day of redemption, and will necessarily inherit the promises. We are heirs, in this family, of everlasting salvation.

CHAPTER 13
Of Sanctification

Justification and sanctification must never be confounded, or separated.

1. They, who are once effectually called, and regenerated, having a new heart, and a new spirit created in them, are further sanctified, really and personally, through the virtue of Christ's death and resurrection (1 Cor. 6:11; Acts 20:32; Phil. 3:10; Rom. 6:5–6), by His Word and Spirit dwelling in them (John 17:17; Eph. 5:26; 2 Thess. 2:13): the dominion of the whole body of sin is destroyed (Rom. 6:6, 14), and the several lusts thereof are more and more weakened and mortified (Gal. 5:24; Rom. 8:13); and they are more and more quickened and strengthened in all saving graces (Col. 1:11; Eph. 3:16–19), to the practice of true holiness, without which no man shall see the Lord (2 Cor. 7:1; Heb. 12:14).

Practical sanctification begins with regeneration. Those effectually called, born again by the Spirit, have as a result a new heart and spirit created within them. The new heart repented and believed, but the process of sanctification does not cease at this point. Through the virtue of the death and resurrection of Christ (i.e. the gospel), the individual believer is continually sanctified on a real and personal basis. The instrument of this sanctification is the Word of God and the indwelling Spirit. The result of the sanctifying work is that the dominion of the old man is utterly wasted and destroyed, the old man being understood as the rule or reign of sin. The lusts of remaining sin are gradually weakened and mortified, while the virtues and graces of true Christianity are gradually strengthened. The result is true holiness, lived out in the world. However, if not lived out, this shows a complete lack of saving faith.

Notice that the Confession identifies effectual calling and regeneration as one kind of sanctification. Once they are effectually called and regenerated, they are "further" sanctified. The new heart believed, and that faith was the instrument of justification. But the new heart also continued to be a new heart, and continued to grow in holiness. In this sense, sanctification precedes justification, because it is a kind of sanctification that makes faith (the instrument of justification) possible.

> 2. This sanctification is throughout, in the whole man (1 Thess. 5:23); yet imperfect in this life, there abiding still some remnants of corruption in every part (1 John 1:10; Rom. 7:18, 23; Phil. 3:12); whence ariseth a continual and irreconcilable war, the flesh lusting against the Spirit, and the Spirit against the flesh (Gal. 5:17; 1 Pet. 2:11).

This sanctification is incomplete in one sense, but not in another. The "reach" of sanctifying impulses can touch every part of a man. But it does not touch every part so that this part becomes perfect or complete. No part of a man is untouched; no part of a man is completed. This incomplete sanctification brings about a state of war between the flesh on the one hand and the spirit on the other.

> 3. In which war, although the remaining corruption, for a time, may much prevail (Rom. 7:23); yet, through the continual supply of strength from the sanctifying Spirit of Christ, the regenerate

part doth overcome (Rom. 6:14; 1 John 5:4; Eph. 4:15–16); and so, the saints grow in grace (2 Pet. 3:18; 2 Cor. 3:18), perfecting holiness in the fear of God (2 Cor. 7:1).

The flow of the battle may look grim for a time. True saints may appear to us as to have no grace, when in fact they are merely in a temporary backslidden state. That backslidden state may continue for a time, but in the truly regenerate, the Spirit never ceases His work, and the spiritual aspect of a man will overcome the fleshly aspect of a man. The result, considered overall, is that the saint grows in grace and perfects holiness in the fear of God.

Unit Seven: For Further Study

 Reading Assignments

Hodge, pp. 179–201[Chapters 11–13]

Vincent, pp. 92–99 [Questions 33–35]

Turretin, Vol. 2, pp. 633–636, 689–693 [Sixteenth Topic: Question 1; Seventeenth Topic: Question 1]

Questions on Reading

1. According to Hodge, who receives justification?

2. In what ways are justification and sanctification distinct graces?

3. In what way is faith to be considered alone?

4. According to Vincent, what are the two elements of justification?

5. In what ways are we to be considered children of God?

6. What is the first distinction between justification and sanctification?

7. For Turretin, what is the basic statement of the question concerning justification?

8. Does Turretin believe justification to be eternal?

9. What is the difference between the chastisements that believers and unbelievers undergo?

10. When does justification occur?

UNIT EIGHT

CHAPTER 14
Of Saving Faith

What, then, is *saving* faith?

> 1. The grace of faith, whereby the elect are enabled to believe to the saving of their souls (Heb. 10:39), is the work of the Spirit of Christ in their hearts (2 Cor. 4:13; Eph. 1:17–19; 2:8), and is ordinarily wrought by the ministry of the Word (Rom. 10:14, 17), by which also, and by the administration of the sacraments, and prayer, it is increased and strengthened (1 Pet. 2:2; Acts 20:32; Rom. 4:11; Luke 17:5; Rom. 1:16–17).

The ordinary course of events is this: the Word is preached, and God uses that Word to transform a sinner's heart by the agency of the Holy Spirit. As a result of this transformed heart, the elect are enabled to believe to the saving of their souls. As said earlier, if they could have repented and believed with their old heart, they didn't need a new one. But once this transformation is complete, the Word and resultant faith do not disappear. The Word, along with baptism, the Lord's Supper, and prayer, works to increase and strengthen the faith of the believer. Please note that the grace that is being strengthened by the sacraments here is *saving* grace. The work following conversion has much in common with the work of conversion.

2. By this faith, a Christian believeth to be true whatsoever is revealed in the Word, for the authority of God Himself speaking therein (John 4:42; 1 Thess. 2:13; 1 John 5:10; Acts 24:14); and acteth differently upon that which each particular passage thereof containeth; yielding obedience to the commands (Rom. 16:26), trembling at the threatenings (Isa. 66:2), and embracing the promises of God for this life, and that which is to come (Heb. 11:13; 1 Tim. 4:8). But the principal acts of saving faith are accepting, receiving, and resting upon Christ alone for justification, sanctification, and eternal life, by virtue of the covenant of grace (John 1:12; Acts 16:31; Gal. 2:20; Acts 15:11).

The faith which is worked in us by the Spirit causes us to believe as true anything revealed in the Bible. This is done because the quickened individual sees the authority of God Himself in the Scriptures. But although God is always the one speaking, He does not always say the same thing. In some passages, He threatens, causing the faithful to tremble. He commands, causing the faithful to seek the way of obedience. In other places, He promises, causing the faithful to trust in the promises for eternal life, as well as the present life. But the center place is occupied with the Word which brings us to accept, receive, and rest upon Christ alone for our justification, sanctification, and eternal life. All this is done under the terms of the covenant of grace, set forth in the Scriptures.

And note that the "principal acts" of saving faith include trusting Christ alone for sanctification. Trusting Christ alone for justification and eternal life seem to us like "converting" motions of faith. But the Westminster divines were very clear that one of the central things done by saving faith is to trust Christ for sanctification. Put another way, if it is not trusting Christ alone for sanctification, then it is not saving faith.

3. This faith is different in degrees, weak or strong (Heb. 5:13–14; Rom. 4:19–20; Matt. 6:30; 8:10); may be often and many ways

assailed, and weakened, but gets the victory (Luke 22:31–32; Eph. 6:16; 1 John 5:4–5): growing up in many to the attainment of a full assurance, through Christ (Heb. 6:11–12; 10:22; Col. 2:2), who is both the author and finisher of our faith (Heb. 12:2).

This faith is not to be understood as a standard unit of divine manufacture. Rather, it is like an organic plant. Apples come in different sizes and shapes, while remaining apples, in a way that ball bearings do not. If it is alive, it will grow up into full assurance of faith at some point, whether in this life or the life to come. But while in this life, the faith in one man may look quite different from the faith in another man. Faith admits of degrees, and may be weak or strong, great or small, triumphant or cautious. But regardless, genuine faith gets the victory.

CHAPTER 15
Of Repentance Unto Life

Repentance is obviously related to the way we behave, and yet it is to be understood as an *evangelical* grace.

> 1. Repentance unto life is an evangelical grace (Zech 12:10; Acts 11:18), the doctrine whereof is to be preached by every minister of the Gospel, as well as that of faith in Christ (Luke 24:47; Mark 1:15; Acts 20:21).

Ministers of Christ are not just to preach faith in Christ; they must also preach repentance unto life. But they are not only to preach repentance, but they are to declare it as an *evangelical* grace. That is, repentance is a gift from God, and is in no way an autonomous offering that we give to Him. He gives it to us. God demands nothing of sinners in salvation which He does not also offer, in the preaching of the Word, as a free gift.

> 2. By it, a sinner, out of the sight and sense not only of the danger, but also of the filthiness and odiousness of his sins, as contrary to the holy nature, and righteous law of God; and upon the apprehension of His mercy in Christ to such as are penitent, so grieves for, and hates his sins, as to turn from them all unto God (Ezek. 18:30–31; 36:31; Isa. 30:22; Ps. 51:4; Jer. 31:18–19; Joel 2:12–13;

Amos 5:15; Ps. 119:128; 2 Cor. 7:11), purposing and endeavour-
ing to walk with Him in all the ways of His commandments (Ps.
119:6, 59, 106; Luke 1:6; 2 Ki. 23:25).

The sinner begins in a state of moral stupidity. He does not see
the danger of his sins, and he does not see the filthiness of them.
He does not do so because he does not connect his behavior to the
holy nature of God, as being inconsistent with who God is and what
God has said. Nor does he see and understand how God would be
delighted to show him mercy if in a state of penitence. If he were to
see this, he would grieve for his sins and hate them, and turn away
from them to God. If brought to this state of repentance, he would
turn to God with the full intent of walking with Him through all his
days, following all His laws.

> 3. Although repentance be not to be rested in, as any satisfac-
> tion for sin, or any cause of the pardon thereof (Ezek. 36:31–32;
> 16:61–63), which is the act of God's free grace in Christ (Hos.
> 14:2, 4; Rom. 3:24; Eph. 1:7); yet it is of such necessity to all sin-
> ners, that none may expect pardon without it (Luke 13:3, 5; Acts
> 17:30–31).

Repentance is necessary to salvation but must never be thought
of as the cause of it. Apples are necessary to the identity of apple
trees, but apples never caused anything to become an apple tree. No
man was ever saved apart from repentance, but repentance is not
the reason God saves him—it is one of the instruments of salvation,
as well as one of the results of it. The so-called "Lordship" contro-
versy in fundamentalist circles is a result of not understanding this
truth. If a man must repent in order to be saved, and if repentance
is not an evangelical gift, then it follows that to demand repentance
is to demand salvation by works. But the problem is in the premises.
Repentance is a gift of God.

4. As there is no sin so small, but it deserves damnation (Rom. 6:23; 5:12; Matt. 12:36); so there is no sin so great, that it can bring damnation upon those who truly repent (Isa. 55:7; Rom. 8:1; Isa. 1:16, 18).

A tiny sin is worthy to damn a man. And by the same token, no sin is so great as to exclude a man from God's presence if there is true repentance. God can and does save the greatest of sinners.

5. Men ought not to content themselves with a general repentance, but it is every man's duty to endeavor to repent of his particular sins, particularly (Ps. 19:13; Luke 19:8; 1 Tim. 1:13, 15).

While there is no obligation to name every particular sin ever committed (which cannot be done), for the sake of simple honesty, it is important for a man to name particular sins as he comes in repentance to God. If he does not, then the possibility is great that his repentance is for sins defined according to his own lights, and not according to the Word. The duty is not to list every last sin, but to list sins in truth without hedging, in a manner that demonstrates that he knows what he is doing.

6. As every man is bound to make private confession of his sins to God, praying for the pardon thereof (Ps. 51:4–5, 7, 9, 14; Ps. 32:5–6); upon which, and the forsaking of them, he shall find mercy (Prov. 28:13; 1 John 1:9); so, he that scandalizeth his brother, or the Church of Christ, ought to be willing, by a private or public confession, and sorrow for his sin, to declare his repentance to those that are offended (James 5:16; Luke 17:3–4; Josh. 7:19; Ps 51), who are thereupon to be reconciled to him, and in love to receive him (2 Cor. 2:8).

Repentance for sin ought to be as public as the sin was, or in some measure commensurate with it. In other words, the duty of repentance brings with it the duty of restitution, whether done publicly or privately as the case may require. When this is done, the sinner is to be received back into fellowship in love.

CHAPTER 16
Of Works

It might seem odd to us that good works are regarded with so much suspicion. Who could be against good works? But if we consider the issue carefully, we will see why there is cause for concern.

> 1. Good works are only such as God hath commanded in His holy Word (Micah 6:8; Rom. 12:2; Heb. 13:21), and not such as, without the warrant thereof, are devised by men, out of blind zeal, or upon any pretense of good intention (Matt. 15:9; Isa. 29:13; 1 Pet. 1:18; Rom. 10:2; John 16:2; 1 Sam. 15:21–23).

If we are to be truly free, we must be bound to the laws and words of God. This is because the only alternative to submission to Christ is submission to Christless men. We must therefore refuse to define good works according to the wisdom of man. These things can indeed have an appearance of wisdom, but are of no value in checking the indulgence of the flesh. The wit of autonomous man does not have the strength to devise a good work.

> 2. These good works, done in obedience to God's commandments, are the fruits and evidences of a true and lively faith (James 2:18, 22): and by them believers manifest their thankfulness (Ps.

116:12–13; 1 Pet. 2:9), strengthen their assurance (1 John 2:3, 5; 2 Pet. 1:5–10), edify their brethren (2 Cor. 9:2; Matt. 5:16), adorn the profession of the gospel (Titus 2:5, 9–12; 1 Tim. 6:1), stop the mouths of the adversaries (1 Pet. 2:15), and glorify God (1 Pet. 2:12; Phil. 1:11; John 15:8), whose workmanship they are, created in Christ Jesus thereunto (Eph. 2:10), that, having their fruit unto holiness, they may have the end, eternal life (Rom. 6:22).

These good works are not the ground of salvation, but they are the ground of *assurance* of salvation. They are the fruit of the tree, not the cause of the tree. They are the clear evidence that the tree is alive and growing. They are fruit and evidence of a true and lively faith. Good works are instruments through which believers show how thankful they are. This also has the result of fortifying assurance of salvation. Good works are a blessing and edification to other believers, and unbelievers see in the good works an adornment to the gospel itself. Those nonbelievers still disposed to kick against the faith are shut down by our good works. All our works together, in all their relations and effects, have the end result of glorifying God. This is because our works are ultimately His works, and when we do them, He is glorified for doing them. The end of the tale is eternal life.

3. Their ability to do good works is not at all of themselves, but wholly from the Spirit of Christ (John 15:4–6; Ezek. 36:26–27). And that they may be enabled thereunto, beside the graces they have already received, there is required an actual influence of the same Holy Spirit, to work in them to will, and to do, of His good pleasure (Phil. 2:13; 4:13; 2 Cor. 3:5): yet are they not hereupon to grow negligent, as if they were not bound to perform any duty unless upon a special motion of the Spirit; but they ought to be diligent in stirring up the grace of God that is in them (Phil. 2:12; Heb. 6:11–12; 2 Pet. 1:3, 5, 10–11; Isa. 64:7; 2 Tim. 1:6; Acts 26:6–7; Jude 20–21).

We are called to work out only what God has worked in. We are dependent upon Him in two senses. First, we depend upon the initial grace that He has given us, but we are also dependent upon the present prompting of the Spirit to particular good deeds—what we might call a "burden." This does not mean we may sit around the house waiting for a burden from the Lord, but rather that we should seek to stir up the grace of God so that we recover any burdens we may have lost.

> 4. They who, in their obedience, attain to the greatest height which is possible in this life, are so far from being able to supererogate, and to do more than God requires, as that they fall short of much which in duty they are bound to do (Luke 17:10; Neh. 13:22; Job 9:2–3; Gal 5:17).

There is no such thing as working above and beyond the call of duty. When we have done all, we should say that we are unworthy servants and did only what we were told. Works of supererogation are defined as works which generate a surplus of virtue, to be put in a grace bank and then used by others. In the Roman system, works of supererogation were added to the merits of Christ in some great spiritual reservoir, and supplicants could draw upon them. This system is what we deny.

> 5. We cannot by our best works merit pardon of sin, or eternal life at the hand of God, by reason of the great disproportion that is between them and the glory to come; and the infinite distance that is between us and God, whom, by them, we can neither profit, nor satisfy for the debt of our former sins (Rom. 3:20; 4:2, 4, 6; Eph. 2:8–9; Titus 3:5–7; Rom. 8:18; Ps. 16:2; Job 22:2–3; 35:7–8), but when we have done all we can, we have done but our duty, and are unprofitable servants (Luke 17:10): and because, as they are good, they proceed from His Spirit (Gal. 5:22–23); and as they are wrought by us, they are defiled, and mixed with so much weakness

and imperfection, that they cannot endure the severity of God's judgment (Isa. 64:6; Gal. 5:17; Rom. 7:15, 18; Ps. 143:2; 130:3).

Our good works must in no way be considered by us as a basis or ground of any good we might receive, whether in this world or the next. Any merit in the works must be attributed to God, and any defilement in the work must be attributed to us.

6. Notwithstanding, the persons of believers being accepted through Christ, their good works also are accepted in Him (Eph. 1:6; 1 Pet. 2:5; Exod 28:38; Gen. 4:4; Heb. 11:4); not as though they were in this life wholly unblamable and unreproveable in God's sight (Job 9:20; Ps. 143:2); but that He, looking upon them in His Son, is pleased to accept and reward that which is sincere, although accompanied with many weaknesses and imperfections (Heb. 13:20–21; 2 Cor. 8:12; Heb. 6:10; Matt. 25:21, 23).

My good works are justified right along with the rest of me. This means that God receives my actions and my life as well as my person, for the sake of the righteousness of Jesus Christ. This means, in short, that my sanctification is justified—which is why it is not rejected by God.

7. Works done by unregenerate men, although for the matter of them they may be things which God commands; and of good use both to themselves and others (2 Ki. 10:30–31; 1 Ki. 21:27, 29; Phil. 1:15–16, 18): yet, because they proceed not from an heart purified by faith (Gen. 4:5; Heb. 11:4, 6); nor are done in a right manner, according to the Word (1 Cor. 13:3; Isa. 1:12); nor to a right end, the glory of God (Matt. 6:2, 5, 16), they are therefore sinful, and cannot please God, or make a man meet to receive grace from God (Hag. 2:14; Titus 1:15; Amos 5:21–22; Hosea 1:4; Rom. 9:16; Titus 3:15): and yet, their neglect of them is more sinful and displeasing unto God (Ps. 14:4; 36:3; Job 21:14–15; Matt. 25:41–43, 45; 23:3).

The unregenerate can do certain works which, considered in themselves, are good. But this is to consider them out of their context. These good works do not commend a man to God in any way, but it would be a more grievous sin to neglect these works, making judgment more severe.

The context of the work empties it of any worth it might have. The work does not proceed from a purified heart, it is not done the way the Bible requires, and it is not directed to the final and ultimate glory of God. The context matters fundamentally. The fact that the piano player in a whorehouse plays good music and plays it well does not alter the context. The fact that a pirate crew might have an enforced code of honor among themselves (admirable in isolation) does not change what the pirate ship is out there doing.

Unit Eight: For Further Study

 Reading Assignments

Hodge, pp. 202–219 [Chapters 14–15]

Vincent, pp. 223–233 [Questions 84–87]

 Questions on Reading

1. According to Hodge, what is spontaneously exercised by all men?

2. How does saving faith come about?

3. What are the two components of saving faith according to Hodge?

4. What is the essence of repentance?

5. Is repentance a cause for pardon of sin?

6. According to Vincent, what does God require of us that we may escape His wrath?

7. How does God work saving faith into the soul?

8. Can any repent in the power of nature?

9. What is hatred of sin?

10. Is obedience required in the new covenant?

UNIT NINE

CHAPTER 17
Of the Perseverance of the Saints

We now come to the one aspect of Calvinism that is actually *popular*. A lot of people like how the fruit tastes, but don't like the tree. They think the fruit delectable, but the bark is ugly.

> 1. They, whom God hath accepted in His Beloved, effectually called, and sanctified by His Spirit, can neither totally nor finally fall away from the state of grace, but shall certainly persevere therein to the end, and be eternally saved (Phil. 1:6; 2 Pet. 1:10; John 10:28–29; 1 John 3:9; 1 Pet. 1:5, 9).

All who are truly called by God will not fail to persevere to the end. This does not apply to those who *claim* to have been effectually called, or who are in visible covenant with God, but it most certainly applies to the genuinely regenerate. Holding to the perseverance of the saints does not mean that we hold to the final perseverance of every covenant member. We hold to the final perseverance of those who are genuinely converted to God. The doctrine could better be called the perseverance of the elect.

> 2. This perseverance of the saints depends not upon their own free will, but upon the immutability of the decree of election, flowing

from the free and unchangeable love of God the Father (2 Tim.
2:18–19; Jer. 31:3); upon the efficacy of the merit and intercession of Jesus Christ (Heb. 10:10, 14; 13:20–21; 9:12–15; Rom.
8:33–39; John 17:11, 24; Luke 22:32; Heb. 7:25), the abiding of
the Spirit, and of the seed of God within them (John 14:16–17;
I John 2:27; 3:9), and the nature of the covenant of grace (Jer.
32:40): from all which ariseth also the certainty and infallibility
thereof (John 10:28; 2 Thess. 3:3; 1 John 2:19).

While the doctrine is called perseverance of the saints (for that
is what the *true* saints do), this fruit is not grounded in the choices
or free will of the saints. It is revealed there, but does not originate
there. Rather, perseverance arises from the work of the triune God
in salvation—the free election of the Father, the potency of the
Son's passion and prayers, and the presence and sustaining power
of the Holy Spirit. In addition, the seed of God is within the elect,
and it will grow to fruition. The fulfillment of the covenant of grace
in the lives of the elect is not a matter of contingencies. From all
this, we know that men who are once effectually called are always
effectually called.

3. Nevertheless, they may, through the temptations of Satan and
of the world, the prevalency of corruption remaining in them,
and the neglect of the means of their preservation, fall into grievous sins (Matt. 26:70, 72, 74); and, for a time, continue therein
(Ps. 51:14): whereby they incur God's displeasure (Isa. 64:5, 7,9;
2 Sam. 11:27), and grieve His Holy Spirit (Eph. 4:30), come to
be deprived of some measure of their graces and comforts (Ps.
51:8, 10, 12; Rev. 2:4; Song 5:2–4, 6), have their hearts hardened
(Isa. 63:17; Mark 6:52; 16:14), and their consciences wounded
(Ps. 32:3–4; 51:8); hurt and scandalize others (2 Sam. 12:14),
and bring temporal judgments upon themselves (Ps. 89:31–32;
1 Cor. 11:32).

But all is not sunshine. The elect may stumble and fall, and many of them do. Because of external temptations from Satan and the world, and internal corruptions like lust and laziness, the elect may fall into gross sin. Further, they may continue in their rebellion for a time. During such times, they bring down on their own heads the displeasure of God and the grief of the Holy Spirit. They cannot continue to enjoy the blessings associated with the Christian faith while in such a state. They have their comforts and graces taken from them. They find themselves hardened for a time. They wound their own consciences—which means that their consciences cannot function as they ought to. They hurt others in the faith, and they set themselves up for temporal chastisements. They, being elect, are not vulnerable to eternal punishment, but the discipline meted out in this life can be severe.

CHAPTER 18
Of Assurance of Grace and Salvation

There is salvation itself, and there is knowledge of salvation. These are quite different things.

> 1. Although hypocrites and other unregenerate men may vainly deceive themselves with false hopes and carnal presumptions of being in the favor of God, and estate of salvation (Job 8:13–14; Micah 3:11; Deut. 29:19; John 8:41) (which hope of theirs shall perish) (Matt. 7:22–23): yet such as truly believe in the Lord Jesus, and love Him in sincerity, endeavouring to walk in all good conscience before Him, may, in this life, be certainly assured that they are in the state of grace (1 John 2:3; 3:14, 18, 19, 21, 24; 5:13), and may rejoice in the hope of the glory of God, which hope shall never make them ashamed (Rom. 5:2, 5).

The doctrine of perseverance is not one that may legitimately be used to comfort the unsaved. A debate over whether diamonds can be lost is no debate at all for a man who has no diamonds but only a clenched fist containing driveway gravel. Vain hypocrites and unregenerate professors have nothing but a false hope. They think they are in the favor of God, and they believe they have entered into the state of salvation. All their hopes shall die along with them.

But those who genuinely believe in Christ, and truly love Him, and who walk before Him with a clean conscience, may comfort themselves with an assurance that God will receive them at the last. This is a basis for strong joy, and such men will never be ashamed. This is not a weak hope, but rather a settled assurance.

> 2. This certainty is not a bare conjectural and probable persuasion grounded upon a fallible hope (Heb. 6:11, 19); but an infallible assurance of faith founded upon the divine truth of the promises of salvation (Heb. 6:17–18), the inward evidence of those graces unto which these promises are made (2 Pet. 1:4–5, 10–11; 1 John 2:3; 3:14; 2 Cor. 1:12), the testimony of the Spirit of adoption witnessing with our spirits that we are the children of God (Rom. 8:15–16), which Spirit is the earnest of our inheritance, whereby we are sealed to the day of redemption (Eph. 1:13–14; 4:30; 2 Cor. 1:21–22).

This is not a hope generated by men on the basis of a line of reasoning they have undertaken on their own authority. Rather, the assurance of the faithful is a work of grace. As such it is infallible. The hope is as secure as the promise upon which it is based. In addition, because the promises were not made to all and everyone, the hope is based upon an inward realization of the graces to which God spoke His promise—the fundamental grace being faith. Further, the Holy Spirit is a Spirit of adoption, and His work includes that of witnessing to our Spirit that we are in fact the children of God. As the earnest of our inheritance, this means that if a true child of God were to be lost and go to hell, then the Spirit would be forfeited as an earnest payment, and would accompany him there. Since this is clearly absurd, we know that someone who has this internal sealing of the Spirit cannot be lost.

> 3. This infallible assurance does not so belong to the essence of faith, but that a true believer may wait long, and conflict with

many difficulties, before he be partaker of it (1 John 5:13; Isa. 1:10; Mark 9:24; Ps. 88; 77:1–12): yet, being enabled by the Spirit to know the things which are freely given him of God, he may, without extraordinary revelation, in the right use of ordinary means, attain thereunto (1 Cor. 2:12; 1 John 4:13; Heb. 6:11–12; Eph. 3:17–19). And therefore it is the duty of every one to give all diligence to make his calling and election sure (2 Pet. 1:10), that thereby his heart may be enlarged in peace and joy in the Holy Ghost, in love and thankfulness to God, and in strength and cheerfulness in the duties of obedience (Rom. 5:1–2, 5; 14:17; 15:13; Eph. 1:3–4; Ps. 4:6–7; Ps. 119:32), the proper fruits of this assurance; so far is it from inclining men to looseness (1 John 2:1–2; Rom. 6:1–2; Titus 2:11–12, 14; 2 Cor. 7:1; Rom. 8:1, 12; 1 John 3:2–3; Ps. 130:4; 1 John 1:6–7).

This assurance is normative, but is not part of the essence of saving faith. This means that a man who doubts his salvation may not use those doubts as *prima facie* evidence that he is in fact unsaved. A genuine believer may go through many trials of assurance before he enjoys the grace of this assurance. Coming to this assurance does not require an extraordinary revelation from the Spirit of God; he should receive this assurance through ordinary means. Those ordinary means would be ordinary means of grace. Assurance of salvation, making one's calling and election sure, is a Christian duty. The result of this would be a heart enlarged in peace and joy given by the Holy Spirit, as well as love and thankfulness to God. Obedience would cease to be a chore, and become rather something conducted in strength and cheerfulness. All these things are a consequence of assurance, and it is very important to note that a biblical assurance is never an encouragement to looseness or laxity of life.

4. True believers may have the assurance of their salvation divers ways shaken, diminished, and intermitted; as, by negligence in

preserving of it, by falling into some special sin which woundeth the conscience and grieveth the Spirit; by some sudden or vehement temptation, by God's withdrawing the light of His countenance, and suffering even such as fear Him to walk in darkness and to have no light (Song 5:2–3, 6; Ps. 51:8, 12, 14; Eph. 4:30–31; Ps. 77:1–10; Matt. 26:69–72; Ps. 31:22; Ps. 88; Isa. 1:10): yet are they never utterly destitute of that seed of God, and life of faith, that love of Christ and the brethren, that sincerity of heart, and conscience of duty, out of which, by the operation of the Spirit, this assurance may, in due time, be revived (1 John 3:9; Luke 22:32; Job 13:15; Ps. 73:15; 51:8, 12; Isa. 1:10); and by the which, in the mean time, they are supported from utter despair (Micah 7:7–9; Jer. 32:40; Isa. 54:7–10; Ps. 22:1; Ps. 88:1).

The elect may lose their assurance in varying degrees. Their assurance may be rattled, lessened, or interrupted. This might come about because they took it for granted and did not preserve it—because they had assurance, they did not think that maintaining it was a duty. They may also lose assurance because of some notable sin which gives ground for self-accusation. With the Spirit grieved, the answers to the accusation are not forthcoming. They may lose assurance because of a vehement assault on their assurance. In other words, loss of assurance may not be the result of another sin; the temptation may be to lose assurance. The problem may occur because God withdraws from the believer to test and prove him, seeing if he doubts in the dark what he knew in the light.

Still, despite such losses, the genuine believer is never utterly destitute of the seed of God along with a remnant of saving faith. These things are not so declined as to make it impossible for a true Christian life to be revived—which means their love for Christ and Christians, sincerity of heart, and sense of duty may be restored. And when they are restored by the Spirit, their assurance will also be restored. And between the loss of assurance and the restoration, the Holy Spirit takes care to see that the believer is not crushed under the weight of complete despair.

Unit Nine: For Further Study

 Reading Assignments

Hodge, pp. 232–247 [Chapters 17–18]

Vincent, pp. 99–102 [Question 36]

Questions on Reading

1. According to Hodge, to whom does the promise of perseverance belong?

2. What is not promised to the true believer?

3. Where is our certainty to be grounded?

4. How do unregenerate men frequently indulge themselves?

5. Is an infallible assurance of the very essence of faith?

6. For Vincent, what is the first of five benefits that belong to justified persons?

7. What is the fifth?

8. Who assuredly attains to the heavenly inheritance?

9. What is true of genuine believers who fall into sin?

10. What is true of those who do fall totally and finally from grace?

UNIT TEN

CHAPTER 19
Of the Law of God

The issue of the law is one of the thorniest questions the church has ever had to work through.

> 1. God gave to Adam a law, as a covenant of works, by which He bound him and all his posterity, to personal, entire, exact, and perpetual obedience, promised life upon the fulfilling, and threatened death upon the breach of it, and endued him with power and ability to keep it (Gen. 1:26–27; 2:17; Rom. 2:14–15; 10:5; 5:12, 19; Gal. 3:10, 12; Eccl. 7:29; Job 28:28).

This covenant in our circles is called the "covenant of creation." The "covenant of works" used here is fine if the terms are defined, but the phrase itself is an unhappy one. It leads people to think it carries its own definition on its face, and hence folks think of some sort of salvation by works. This leads people to assume two different ways of salvation—grace and works. But the Westminster theologians here are clearly thinking of a gracious covenant—God "endued him with power and ability to keep it."

There was clearly a covenant in the Garden. A covenant is a solemn bond, sovereignly administered, with attendant blessings and curses. The charge to Adam was certainly solemn, and God administered it by speaking the words of it. He promised that disobedience would bring death and that continued obedience would bring maintained access to the tree of life. This covenant was with Adam and all his posterity. It obligated us to entire obedience, and obligates us still. The fact that it is broken does not mean it ceases to be binding. If a man and a woman commit adultery once, this does not give them permission to continue. The fact that Adam was unfaithful does not mean we have a right to be unfaithful. Another way of expressing this is that outside of Christ we are constantly breaking covenant with God. Our rebellion is ongoing.

> 2. This law, after his fall, continued to be a perfect rule of righteousness; and, as such, was delivered by God upon Mount Sinai, in ten commandments, and written in two tables (James 1:25; 2:8, 10–12; Rom. 13:8–9; Deut. 5:32; 10:4; Exod 24:1): the first four commandments containing our duty towards God; and the other six, our duty to man (Matt. 22:37–40).

The standards of morality did not change as a result of the Fall. Just as the ten commandments are summarized by the two great commandments—love God and love your neighbor—so they are summarized by the one great commandment before the Fall, which was to not eat of the fruit of the tree of knowledge.

The first table of the law, the first four commandments, describe our obligations to God, and the last six describe our obligations to man. This same division is seen in the two great commandments as well: love God and love our neighbor.

> 3. Besides this law, commonly called moral, God was pleased to give to the people of Israel, as a church under age, ceremonial laws, containing several typical ordinances, partly of worship, prefiguring Christ, His graces, actions, sufferings, and benefits (Heb. 9; 10:1; Gal. 4:1–3; Col. 2:17); and partly, holding forth divers

instructions of moral duties (1 Cor. 5:7; 2 Cor. 6:17; Jude 23). All which ceremonial laws are now abrogated, under the new testament (Col. 2:14, 16–17; Dan. 9:27; Eph. 2:15–16).

The common name for this is the moral law, but by this we do not mean that other commandments of God are not moral. In addition to this "moral" law, God gave other requirements to Israel as the immature Church. The ceremonies given to Israel were given as a prefiguration of Christ's person and work, and as such remain a source of instruction for Christians today. Under the New Testament, they do not remain binding on Christians today as ceremonies. They do remain as instruction. Various moral instructions are mixed in with them, and these moral instructions remain binding.

> 4. To them also, as a body politic, He gave sundry judicial laws, which expired together with the State of that people; not obliging any other now, further than the general equity thereof may require (Exod. 21; 22:1–29; Gen. 49:10; 1 Pet. 2:13–14; Matt. 5:17, 38–39; 1 Cor. 9:8–10).

God gave Israel particular judicial laws. A particular command at a particular time does not necessarily extend to others. The fact that God commanded Israel to invade Canaan does not require us to invade Canaan. At the same time, the fact that God was the one speaking these commands should make us take note. We are required to reason by analogy, and extend the general equity of the law to our situations. For example, God required a parapet around the roofs of houses, and a man was guilty of culpable negligence if someone fell off his roof because a parapet was not there. We do not spend time on our roofs, as they did, and so the requirement as such does not apply to us. But the general equity does bind us, and we are required to put a deck rail around a second-story deck.

This should remind us of the vast difference between "top down" approaches to civil law (Justinian) and "historical, linear" approaches to civil law, i.e. common law. In many cases, people are afraid of theonomy or theocracy because they assume it to be the former and not the latter. But the theonomic or theocratic system is a case law system, a common law system. King Alfred established common law for his people by applying the law of Deuteronomy to his people—but he did not just apply the *standards*, he also applied the *method*.

> 5. The moral law doth for ever bind all, as well justified persons as others, to the obedience thereof (Rom. 13:8–10; Eph. 6:2; 1 John 2:3–4, 7–8); and that, not only in regard of the matter contained in it, but also in respect of the authority of God the Creator, who gave it (James 2:10–11). Neither doth Christ, in the Gospel, any way dissolve, but much strengthen this obligation (Matt. 5:17–19; James 2:8; Rom. 3:31).

The moral law and the moral aspects of all other laws are perpetually binding on all men, Christian and non-Christian alike. We are bound by the moral law proper: we must love the Lord our God with all our hearts, souls, minds, and strength. We are bound by the moral law when it is mixed in with ceremonial requirements: we must keep the festival of Passover by ridding ourselves of the yeast of malice and wickedness. We are bound by those aspects of the moral law visible in the particular judicial requirements given to Israel: we must not allow women in combat because it is not right to boil a kid in the mother goat's milk.

We are not under law but under grace (Rom. 6:14). This means that sin shall not be our master. Being under grace does not mean that we now "get" to sin; it means we have been liberated from it, with the definition of sin remaining what it has been through all ages—lawlessness.

6. Although true believers be not under the law, as a covenant of works, to be thereby justified, or condemned (Rom. 6:14; Gal. 2:16; 3:13; 4:4–5; Acts 13:39; Rom. 8:1); yet is it of great use to them, as well as to others; in that, as a rule of life informing them of the will of God, and their duty, it directs and binds them to walk accordingly (Rom. 7:12, 22, 25; Ps. 119:4–6; 1 Cor. 7:19; Gal. 5:14, 16, 18–23); discovering also the sinful pollutions of their nature, hearts, and lives (Rom. 7:7; 3:20); so as, examining themselves thereby, they may come to further conviction of, humiliation for, and hatred against sin (James 1:23–25; Rom. 7:9, 14, 24), together with a clearer sight of the need they have of Christ, and the perfection of His obedience (Gal. 3:24; Rom. 7:24–25; 8:3–4). It is likewise of use to the regenerate, to restrain their corruptions, in that it forbids sin (James 2:11; Ps. 119:101, 104, 128): and the threatenings of it serve to show what even their sins deserve; and what afflictions, in this life, they may expect for them, although freed from the curse thereof threatened in the law (Ezra 9:13–14; Ps. 89:30–34). The promises of it, in like manner, shew them God's approbation of obedience, and what blessings they may expect upon the performance thereof (Lev. 26:1–14; 2 Cor. 6:16; Eph. 6:2–3; Ps. 37:11; Matt. 5:5; Ps. 19:11): although not as due to them by the law as a covenant of works (Gal. 2:16; Luke 17:10). So as, a man's doing good, and refraining from evil, because the law encourageth to the one and detereth from the other, is no evidence of his being under the law; and not under grace (Rom. 6:12, 14; 1 Pet. 3:8–12; Ps. 34:12–16; Heb. 12:28–29).

We come now to one of the three legitimate uses of the law, which is a different thing entirely from the three types of law. The first use discussed here is the help the law provides to the regenerate, informing and teaching him. (The other two uses are restraint of the godless and as a means of evangelism.) But first, in the minds of the godly, we must consider how the law is not to be used. The law is not, and cannot be, a ladder by which men climb to heaven. It is not a means of justification or sanctification. It is a standard of righteousness, not a means to righteousness. With this clear, how may a gracious believer use the law?

First, it teaches the believer what God's will is. Secondly, it teaches the believer how many sinful pollutions remain in him, which need to be attended to by the grace of God. This drives him to a greater understanding of the need for Christ, just as it does with a non-believer who is being drawn into the kingdom. Third, it helps the godly to understand what their sins deserve—and not just the fact that their sins are sinful. In short, they are helped to see the magnitude of sin. Conversely, they see the fruitfulness of obedience in the promises of the law. We do not claim the promises of the law as though we had kept the covenant of works in Adam, but we claim them by faith as our portion under the covenant of grace, given in the second Adam.

In all this, we cannot say that if a man obeys the law that he is somehow, in Paul's sense "under the law," and not under grace. Legalism is not to be confounded with obedience. If obedience is legalism, then disobedience must be obedience.

> 7. Neither are the forementioned uses of the law contrary to the grace of the Gospel, but do sweetly comply with it (Gal. 3:21); the Spirit of Christ subduing and enabling the will of man to do that freely, and cheerfully, which the will of God, revealed in the law, requireth to be done (Ezek. 36:27; Heb. 8:10; Jer. 31:33).

Do we set aside the law in all this emphasis on grace? Not at all; rather we uphold the law.

CHAPTER 20
Of Christian Liberty, and Liberty of Conscience

If this is our relation to law, what room is there for liberty?

1. The liberty which Christ hath purchased for believers under the Gospel consists in their freedom from the guilt of sin, the condemning wrath of God, the curse of the moral law (Titus 2:14; 1 Thess. 1:10; Gal. 3:13); and, in their being delivered from this present evil world, bondage to Satan, and dominion of sin (Gal. 1:4; Col. 1:13; Acts 26:18; Rom. 6:14); from the evil of afflictions, the sting of death, the victory of the grave, and everlasting damnation (Rom. 8:28; Ps. 119:71; 1 Cor. 15:54–57; Rom. 8:1); as also, in their free access to God (Rom. 5:1–2), and their yielding obedience unto Him, not out of slavish fear, but a child–like love and willing mind (Rom. 8:14–15; 1 John 4:18). All which were common also to believers under the law (Gal. 3:9, 14). But, under the new testament, the liberty of Christians is further enlarged, in their freedom from the yoke of the ceremonial law, to which the Jewish Church was subjected (Gal. 4:1–3, 6–7; 5:1; Acts 15:10–11); and in greater boldness of access to the throne of grace (Heb. 4:14, 16; Heb. 10:19–22), and in fuller communications of the free Spirit of God, than believers under the law did ordinarily partake of (John 7:38–39; 2 Cor. 3:13, 17–18).

First, it is important for us to see this section following right after the teaching on the law of God. The law of God sets the boundaries within which we may exercise our liberty. Having set this context, the Confession goes on to define what our liberty is—a very important thing to do. If we assume that we know what we mean by liberty, hidden definitions will plague our discussion.

Liberty means, first, freedom from guilt, God's judgment, and the condemnation of moral law. It also means we are delivered from the wickedness of the world, the hatred of Satan, and the dominion of sin. We are also freed from the consequences of such things—the evil of afflictions, fear of death, the dominion of death, and Hell.

We are also freed *to* certain things—we are free to approach God and free to obey Him from love and willingness, not from fear. In these respects, we are like our brothers in the Old Testament.

But our liberty is greater than theirs. We are freed from the ceremonial requirements of the law, and we have a more abundant display of God's grace upon us than they did. Note in this that "liberty" always implies a standard, and this standard always brings with it an antithesis. This means that he who says "free from" must also assert a specified "free to." Liberty always necessitates, therefore, an appeal to a source of law.

> 2. God alone is Lord of the conscience (James 4:12; Rom. 14:4), and hath left it free from the doctrines and commandments of men, which are, in any thing, contrary to His Word; or beside it, in matters of faith, or worship (Acts 4:19; 5:29; 1 Cor. 7:23; Matt. 23:8–10; 2 Cor. 1:24; Matt. 15:9). So that, to believe such doctrines, or to obey such commands, out of conscience, is to betray true liberty of conscience (Col. 2:20, 22–23; Gal. 1:10; 2:4–5; 5:1): and the requiring of an implicit faith, and an absolute and blind obedience, is to destroy liberty of conscience, and reason also (Rom. 10:17; 14:23; Isa. 8:20; Acts 17:11; John 4:22; Hos. 5:11; Rev. 13:12, 16–17; Jer. 8:9).

Because God is our Lord, He alone is Lord of the conscience. This means that, in matters of faith and worship, men cannot command us in His name when He has not spoken. Obedience to men is certainly permissible, but it is prohibited to obey men as though they had the right to bind the conscience in the same way that God does.

We are required to compare what men say with the Word of God, and may not simply assume that they must have a good biblical reason for teaching what they do. This teaching against "implicit faith" is directly aimed at a doctrine of the Roman church, which required this of those under her authority.

Thus: we are freed from men, and freed to God.

> 3. They who, upon pretence of Christian liberty, do practice any sin, or cherish any lust, do thereby destroy the end of Christian liberty, which is, that being delivered out of the hands of our enemies, we might serve the Lord without fear, in holiness and righteousness before Him, all the days of our life (Gal. 5:13; 1 Pet. 2:16; 2 Pet. 2:19; John 8:34; Luke 1:74–75).

The end or purpose of Christian liberty is the pursuit of holiness. Those who wave the banner of Christian liberty so that they might do whatever they want have not understood the doctrine at all. The point is not to drink or smoke or dance according to your own whims, but to do so before the Lord, with the increase of joy and holiness obvious to all.

> 4. And because the powers which God hath ordained, and the liberty which Christ hath purchased, are not intended by God to destroy, but mutually to uphold and preserve one another, they who, upon pretence of Christian liberty, shall oppose any lawful power, or the lawful exercise of it, whether it be civil or ecclesiastical, resist the ordinance of God (Matt. 12:25; 1 Pet. 2:13–14, 16; Rom. 13:1–8; Heb. 13:17). And, for their publishing of such opinions,

or maintaining of such practices, as are contrary to the light of nature, or to the known principles of Christianity (whether concerning faith, worship, or conversation), or to the power of godliness; or, such erroneous opinions or practices, as either in their own nature, or in the manner of publishing or maintaining them, are destructive to the external peace and order which Christ hath established in the Church, they may lawfully be called to account (Rom. 1:32; 1 Cor. 5:1, 5, 11, 13; 2 John 10–11; 2 Thess. 3:14; 1 Tim. 6:3–5; Titus 1:10–11, 13; 3:10; Matt 18:15–17; 1 Tim. 1:19–20; Rev. 2:2, 14–15, 20; Rev. 3:9), and proceeded against, by the censures of the Church, and by the power of the civil magistrate (Deut 13:6–12; Rom. 13:3–4; 2 John 10–11; Ezra 7:23, 25–28; Rev. 17:12, 16–17; Neh. 13:15, 17, 21–22, 25, 30; 2 Ki. 23:5–6, 9, 20–21; 2 Chron. 34:33; 15:12–13, 16; Dan. 3:29; 1 Tim. 2:2; Isa. 49:23; Zech. 13:2–3).

There are limits (obviously) to civil and ecclesiastical authority, but those limits are not established by the desires of private spirits. A man may withstand them only if he has warrant from the Word of God to do so. If he does not, then he may not. There is an important twofold division. We may not oppose lawful power, and we may not oppose lawful exercise of power. In other words, we must distinguish the two. A lawful power may require an unlawful thing. Not only does Christian liberty not mean antinomianism, it also does not mean anarchy.

According to the Confession, men may live and die as heretics and do so in peace. But if they publish such opinions as are likely to disrupt public order and obedience, or if they publish a particular doctrine in such a way as to bring about that disruption, then they may be called to give an account of themselves. If they do not heed the rebuke, they may be restrained or punished, in keeping with the nature of the offense.

Depending on the offense, the action against them may be taken by the Church, or by the magistrate, or both. The American Presbyterian Church, in a misguided moment, deleted the last phrase which says, "and by the power of the civil magistrate." They did this at their First General Assembly in 1789. The move was misguided because they were assuming that everyone would retain a residual faith in certain basics, whether by the light of nature or by Christian consensus. They could not have foreseen, for example, the butchery of the modern abortion industry.

Unit Ten: For Further Study

 ## Reading Assignments

Hodge, pp. 248–269 [Chapters 19–20]

Vincent, pp. 109–222 [Questions 39–83]

Turretin, Vol. 2, pp. 137–141 [Eleventh Topic: Question 22]

 ## Questions on Reading

1. According to Hodge, in addition to being the natural head of the human race, what was Adam also?

2. How was the moral law summarily comprehended?

3. What is the Christian believer's relationship to the ceremonial law?

4. According to Vincent, what is the rule for our obedience?

5. Does the new covenant abolish the moral law?

6. If the Ten Commandments are the summary of the whole moral law, what summarizes the Ten Commandments?

7. Are all sins equally heinous?

8. According to Turretin, what distinction should be made in the use of the law?

9. What is the difference between them?

10. What are the two ways man is obligated to keep the law?

UNIT ELEVEN

CHAPTER 21
Of Religious Worship, and the Sabbath Day

Our duties before God include the calendar, and so we come to the question of times and days.

1. The light of nature sheweth that there is a God, who hath lord-ship and sovereignty over all, is good, and doth good unto all, and is therefore to be feared, loved, praised, called upon, trusted in, and served, with all the heart, and with all the soul, and with all the might (Rom. 1:20; Acts 17:24; Ps. 119:68; Jer. 10:7; Ps. 31:23; 18:3; Rom. 10:12; Ps. 62:8; Josh. 24:14; Mark 12:33). But the acceptable way of worshipping the true God is instituted by Himself, and so limited by His own revealed will, that He may not be worshipped according to the imaginations and devices of men, or the sugges-tions of Satan, under any visible representation, or any other way not prescribed in the holy Scripture (Deut. 12:32; Matt. 15:9; Acts 17:25; Matt. 4:9–10; Deut. 15:1–20; Exod. 20:4–6; Col. 2:23).

Natural revelation tells us that there is a God, and that He is good. Not only is He good, but His Deity is beyond all majesty, and He is worthy of all worship. The greatest commandment found in Scripture (to love God with all that we have and are) is also found in the stars and forests. Natural revelation tells us of our duty to worship

God, but is silent on the manner of worship which is acceptable to Him. God Himself is the one who must tell us how to worship Him, and so this excludes worship according to the inventions of men, or the lies of the devil. Particularly excluded would be worship through idolatrous images, or rites not prescribed in the Bible.

But as we must discover, a great deal rides on what we mean by "prescribed." Of course, all Protestants must be regulativists of some stripe, worshipping only as God has taught us, but our hermeneutic will determine what and how we are taught. Do we require "express warrant" from the Scriptures, or do we look for direction that goes beyond express warrant? The dangers of an "express warrant" regulativism should become apparent shortly.

> 2. Religious worship is to be given to God, the Father, Son, and Holy Ghost; and to Him alone (Matt. 4:10; John 5:23; 2 Cor. 13:14); not to angels, saints, or any other creature (Col. 2:18; Rev. 19:10; Rom. 1:25): and, since the fall, not without a Mediator; nor in the mediation of any other but of Christ alone (John 14:6; 1 Tim. 2:5; Eph. 2:18; Col. 3:17).

First we must settle whom we worship. The biblical answer is that we worship the triune God, and only the triune God. We must not worship angels or saints, or anyone else who is not God. Further, since the Fall, we must worship by means of a (priestly) mediator. The Son of God would have been the visible image of the invisible Father, fall or no fall, but the presence of sin required the presence of a priest who would deal with the sin. But that mediator (ultimately) cannot be anyone other than the Lord Jesus Christ. The priests under the Old Covenant were not substitutes for Christ, but rather types of Him.

> 3. Prayer, with thanksgiving, being one special part of religious worship (Phil. 4:6), is by God required of all men (Ps. 65:2): and, that it may be accepted, it is to be made in the name of the Son

(John 14:13–14; 1 Pet. 2:5), by the help of His Spirit (Rom. 8:26), according to His will (1 John 5:14), with understanding, reverence, humility, fervency, faith, love and perseverance (Ps. 47:7; Eccl. 5:1–2; Heb. 12:28; Gen. 18:27; James 5:16; 1:6–7; Mark 11:24; Matt. 6:12, 14–15; Col. 4:2; Eph. 6:18); and, if vocal, in a known tongue (1 Cor. 14:14).

Gratitude is one of the first duties of men. God requires it to accompany all prayers, and we must take care to offer our prayers in a way that will be accepted. This means they must be offered up in the name of the Son, with the Spirit enabling and empowering the offering. We must seek to pray in His will, and with all appropriate understanding. We are not to pray in blind faith. Nor are we to pray without reverence, humility, zeal, faith, love and steadfastness. We must always remember when we pray who we are and who God. If we speak aloud in prayer, then we must understand what we say, for we are responsible for it.

> 4. Prayer is to be made for things lawful (1 John 5:14); and for all sorts of men living, or that shall live hereafter (1 Tim. 2:1–2; John 17:20; 2 Sam. 7:29; Ruth 4:12): but not for the dead (2 Sam. 12:21–23; Luke 16:25–26; Rev. 14:13), nor for those of whom it may be known that they have sinned the sin unto death (1 John 5:16).

We may not pray that God's law would be set aside. We may pray for men living, or men who will come to live after us. We may not pray for the dead, as though we are capable of altering their state, or for those known to be reprobate.

> 5. The reading of the Scriptures with godly fear (Acts 15:21; Rev. 1:3), the sound preaching (2 Tim. 4:2) and conscionable hearing of the Word, in obedience unto God, with understanding, faith and reverence (James 1:22; Acts 10:33; Matt. 13:19; Heb. 4:2; Isa. 66:2), singing of psalms with grace in the heart (Col. 3:16; Eph.

5:19; James 5:13); as also, the due administration and worthy receiving of the sacraments instituted by Christ, are all parts of the ordinary religious worship of God (Matt. 28:19; 1 Cor. 11:23–29; Acts 2:42): beside religious oaths (Deut 6:13; Neh. 10:29), vows (Isa. 19:21; Eccl. 5:4–5), solemn fastings (Joel 2:12; Esth. 4:16; Matt. 9:15; 1 Cor. 7:5), and thanksgivings upon special occasions (Ps. 107; Esth. 9:22), which are, in their several times and seasons, to be used in an holy and religious manner (Heb. 12:28).

In the corporate worship of the Church, we should look for those features of religious worship that we find required or described in Scripture. The Bible should be read aloud, with all appropriate reverence. The Word of God should be preached and declared. The hearing of the Word read and preached, with all appropriate understanding, is equally important to sound worship, and shows that the congregation is active in worship, not passive. The Church should sing psalms from the heart and receive those sacraments which have been offered according to the Word.

Occasional duties also arise in worship. They include oaths and vows, fasts and occasional thanksgivings, which are to be observed with all prudence. It is most interesting to note that in defense of the worship on "special occasions" the Westminster theologians cited Esther 9, which tells of the establishment of Purim, a recurring *annual* festival not required by the Mosaic law, and which had no divine authorization from God in the form of express warrant.

6. Neither prayer, nor any other part of religious worship, is now, under the Gospel, either tied unto, or made more acceptable by any place in which it is performed, or towards which it is directed (John 4:21): but God is to be worshipped everywhere (Mal. 1:11; 1 Tim. 2:8), in spirit and truth (John 4:23–24); as, in private families (Jer. 10:25; Deut. 6:6–7; Job 1:5; 2 Sam. 6:18, 20; 1 Pet. 3:7; Acts 10:2), daily (Matt. 6:11), and in secret, each one by himself (Matt. 6:6;

Eph. 6:18); so, more solemnly in the public assemblies, which are not carelessly or willfully to be neglected, or forsaken, when God, by His Word or providence, calleth thereunto (Isa. 56:6–7; Heb. 10:25; Prov. 1:20–21, 24; 8:34; Acts 13:42; Luke 4:16; Acts 2:42).

Under the New Covenant, we cannot say that any particular place is holy ground. Strictly speaking, we cannot have "sanctuaries" now that the Church is the Temple of God. As before, God is to be worshipped in all places, with a right heart and spirit. He may be worshipped on a daily basis, in our households and in private.

The solemnity of public worship receives it dignity from the fact that the living stones of the Temple are calling upon God. The sanctity of our surroundings in worship is derived from the fact of the people of God worshipping there, and not the other way around. Our church buildings set the context of worship, but are no longer part of the content of worship.

The assembling together for worship is on no account to be despised or neglected. God has required it.

> 7. As it is the law of nature, that, in general, a due proportion of time be set apart for the worship of God; so, in His Word, by a positive, moral, and perpetual commandment binding all men in all ages, He hath particularly appointed one day in seven, for a Sabbath, to be kept holy unto him (Exod. 20:8, 10–11; Isa. 56:2, 4, 6–7): which, from the beginning of the world to the resurrection of Christ, was the last day of the week; and, from the resurrection of Christ, was changed into the first day of the week (Gen. 2:2–3; 1 Cor. 16:1–2; Acts 20:7), which, in Scripture, is called the Lord's Day (Rev. 1:10), and is to be continued to the end of the world, as the Christian Sabbath (Exod. 20:8, 10; Matt. 5:17–18).

Natural revelation shows us that a portion of our time must be set aside expressly for the worship of God. Special revelation teaches us that the time necessary for this is one day in seven. Before the coming of Christ, the creation of the world was commemorated and, under the type of the Exodus, the redemption of God's people. After the coming of Christ, the commemoration is of the recreation of the world, the restructuring of the heavens and earth, in the resurrection of Christ. The Sabbath was tied to the *creation*, and nothing would suffice to change the day other than a *new* creation, a new heavens and earth. And that is what we have in the resurrection of Christ, establishing the Lord's Day, the Sabbath of the new earth, the Sabbath of the regeneration (Heb. 4:10).

> 8. This Sabbath is then kept holy unto the Lord, when men, after a due preparing of their hearts, and ordering of their common affairs before–hand, do not only observe an holy rest, all the day, from their own works, words, and thoughts about their worldly employments and recreations (Exod. 20:8; 16:23, 25–26, 29–30; 31:15–17; Isa. 58:13; Neh. 13:15–22), but also are taken up, the whole time, in the public and private exercises of His worship, and in the duties of necessity and mercy (Isa. 58:13; Matt. 12:1–13).

The Sabbath is to be observed just as God has instructed. And this is why we come now to a place where we part company with the teaching of the Confession. We understand the works of piety to be *commanded* for the Sabbath, and works of necessity and mercy to be *permitted*, as occasion requires. In other words, these three different kinds of work are certainly permitted on the Lord's Day. But this is very different from equating these kinds of works with a "holy rest." The Lord did not say to work for six days in one way, and work hard for one day in another way. The central requirement of the Lord's Day is that of rest. In other words, we dispute the legitimacy of the phrase "the whole time." This understanding would exclude resting, which is the heart of the commandment. We may interrupt our rest with worship, or changing an old lady's flat tire, or fixing sandwiches for the guests we invited over after church. But if we are doing things like this "the whole time" on the Sabbath, we will be working seven days out of seven, and we will have become Sabbath-breakers. The law requires napping on the couch in a sun puddle.

The central point made by this section remains constant: right Sabbath-keeping requires preparation of the heart and house.

CHAPTER 22
Of Lawful Oaths and Vows

How should we speak when we are invoking the name of God?

1. A lawful oath is part of religious worship (Deut. 10:20), wherein, upon just occasion, the person swearing solemnly calleth God to witness what he asserteth, or promiseth, and to judge him according to the truth or falsehood of what he sweareth (Exod. 20:7; Lev. 19:12; 2 Cor. 1:23; 2 Chron. 6:22–23).

Not only is an oath lawful, it should be considered an act of worship before God. The essence of an oath lies in calling God as a witness of what is said—invoking Him—as the ultimate judge of the truth or falsity of what is said. As an act of worship, an oath should be taken only upon just and solemn occasions—as in a wedding, or being sworn into membership in a local church.

2. The name of God only is that by which men ought to swear, and therein it is to be used with all holy fear and reverence (Deut. 6:13). Therefore, to swear vainly, or rashly, by that glorious and dreadful Name; or, to swear at all by any other thing, is sinful, and to be abhorred (Exod. 20:7; Jer. 5:7; Matt. 5:34, 37; James 5:12). Yet, as in matters of weight and moment, an oath is warranted by the Word of God, under the new testament as well as under the

old (Heb. 6:16; 2 Cor. 1:23; Isa. 65:16); so a lawful oath, being imposed by lawful authority, in such matters, ought to be taken (1 Ki. 8:31; Neh. 13:25; Ezra 10:5).

When men swear, they are to do so in the name of the living God only. Because this is the only name to be used in a lawful oath, this means that the taking of an oath should be attended with fear and reverence. There are two ways of sinning in manner with an oath. The first is to swear by the name of the great and terrible God, but to do so frivolously. The other is to swear by the name of any other thing. Such things are not only sins, but sins to be abhorred. Nevertheless, when the occasion warrants, in matters that are weighty, an oath is lawful—regardless of the fact that we are under the New Covenant. The New Testament contains numerous occasions of lawful oaths. Therefore, when the occasion is fitting, a proper oath should be taken.

3. Whosoever taketh an oath ought duly to consider the weightiness of so solemn an act, and therein to avouch nothing but what he is fully persuaded is the truth (Exod. 20:7; Jer. 4:2): neither may any man bind himself by oath to any thing but what is good and just, and what he believeth so to be, and what he is able and resolved to perform (Gen. 24:2–3, 5–6, 8–9). **Yet it is a sin to refuse an oath touching any thing that is good and just, being imposed by lawful authority (Num. 5:19, 21; Neh. 5:12; Exod. 22:7–11).**

With regard to the substance of an oath, only what is known to be the truth should be affirmed. Moreover, it is a sin to bind oneself by an oath to do a sinful thing, or to bind oneself to fulfill something he cannot fulfill. One of the great concerns at the time of the Reformation was the question of vows of celibacy which many had taken. When they came out of Rome, were they obligated to continue to try to live in a celibate fashion? The Westminster theologians considered the unmarried state to be unnatural (unless God had given a gift of celibacy).

For regular people, ungifted in this way, a vow of celibacy was sinful and was to be rejected. In addition to this, the original Confession maintained that it was sinful to refuse to take an oath when a lawful authority required it. This is indicated by the sentence in bold, which was deleted by the first American Assembly of 1789.

> 4. An oath is to be taken in the plain and common sense of the words, without equivocation, or mental reservation (Jer. 4:2; Ps. 24:4). It cannot oblige to sin; but in any thing not sinful, being taken, it binds to performance, although to a man's own hurt (1 Sam. 25:22, 32–34; Ps. 15:4). Nor is it to be violated, although made to heretics, or infidels (Ezek. 17:16, 18–19; Josh. 9:18–19; 2 Sam. 21:1).

Oaths are to be interpreted according to a straightforward and honest handling of the words. If a man has bound himself to a sinful condition, the oath does not bind. Examples would include an oath to kill someone, or, as mentioned above, an oath of celibacy when one did not have the gift of celibacy. But if the oath does not bind to a sinful condition, but only to a difficult or grievous one, the oath remains in effect. The authority of the oath is not affected by the spiritual condition of the one to whom the promise was made.

> 5. A vow is of the like nature with a promissory oath, and ought to be made with the like religious care, and to be performed with the like faithfulness (Isa. 19:21; Eccl. 5:4–6; Ps. 61:8; 66:13–14).

The same goes for vows.

> 6. It is not to be made to any creature, but to God alone (Ps. 76:11; Jer. 44:25–26): and that it may be accepted, it is to be made voluntarily, out of faith, and conscience of duty, in way of thankfulness for mercy received, or for the obtaining of what we want, whereby we more strictly bind ourselves to necessary duties: or, to other things, so far and so long as they may fitly conduce

thereunto (Deut 23:21–23; Ps. 50:14; Gen. 28:20–22; 1 Sam. 1:11; Ps. 66:13–14; 132:2–5).

A vow is not to be made to any creature, but only to God. It is a freewill offering, not made under compulsion. The motive force is faith and conscience of duty. The reasons we may pay our vows may be thankfulness for mercy, or for material blessings. When we receive such things, we set up fences for ourselves, in order that we may serve God effectively in our new station.

> 7. No man may vow to do any thing forbidden in the Word of God, or what would hinder any duty therein commanded, or which is not in his own power, and for the performance whereof he hath no promise of ability from God (Acts 23:12, 14; Mark 6:26; Numb. 30:5, 8, 12–13). In which respects, popish monastical vows of perpetual single life, professed poverty, and regular obedience, are so far from being degrees of higher perfection, that they are superstitious and sinful snares, in which no Christian may entangle himself (Matt. 19:11–12; 1 Cor. 7:2, 9; Eph. 4:28; 1 Pet. 4:2; 1 Cor. 7:23).

To reiterate an earlier point, no man may lawfully vow to do an unlawful thing. Nor may he vow to do something which would hinder him in his duties, or make a vow he is unable to perform, and has no reason to suppose that God will enable him to perform it. Specifically, the vows of perpetual celibacy, assumed poverty, and obedience to the standards of a monastic order, are not at all examples of super-spirituality. They are actually superstitions and horrible traps, in which no Christian should remain. A good contemporary example of this kind of vow is the common vow, which many evangelicals have taken, to abstain from any alcoholic beverage in any form. In all such things, the devil is up to his regular tricks ... taking wonderful things away from us.

Unit Eleven: For Further Study

 Reading Assignments

Hodge, pp. 270–283 [Chapter 21]

Vincent, pp. 266–282 [Questions 98–107]

Turretin, Vol. 2, pp. 77–100 [Eleventh Topic: Questions 13–14]

 Questions on Reading

1. How does Hodge describe the regulative principle?

2. Why is it a sin to fail to worship God rightly?

3. What is Hodge's first objection to the worship of saints, angels or Mary?

4. What spirit should and should not attend Sabbath observance?

5. According to Vincent, how many parts are there in prayer?

6. Why must we pray in the name of Christ?

7. What special rule should direct our prayers?

8. According to Turretin, how many different kinds of Sabbath are there?

9. What status does the fourth commandment have, according to Turretin?

10. What is the Lord's Day?

UNIT TWELVE

CHAPTER 23
Of the Civil Magistrate

When we get to the political issues, we get to the point where we are no longer "preaching," but rather are "meddling."

> 1. God, the supreme Lord and King of all the world, hath ordained civil magistrates, to be, under Him, over the people, for His own glory, and the public good: and, to this end, hath armed them with the power of the sword, for the defense and encouragement of them that are good, and for the punishment of evil doers (Rom. 13:1–4; 1 Pet. 2:13–14).

God has established the civil magistrate in two relations. The first is that the magistrate is under Him. The second is that the magistrate is over the people. Scripture gives two reasons for this; the first and greatest is that this glorifies God. The second reason is that the public good is advanced by this arrangement. In order to bring these about, God has armed the magistrate with the power of the sword—lethal violence. In its turn, the sword is to be employed for two purposes and in two directions. The first is the defense and encouragement of good people, and the second is the punishment of the wicked.

> 2. It is lawful for Christians to accept and execute the office of a magistrate, when called thereunto (Prov. 8:15–16; Rom. 13:1–4):

in the managing whereof, as they ought especially to maintain piety, justice, and peace, according to the wholesome laws of each commonwealth (Ps. 2:10–12; 1 Tim. 2:2; Ps. 82:3–4; 2 Sam. 23:3; 1 Pet. 2:13); so, for that end, they may lawfully, now under the new testament, wage war, upon just and necessary occasion (Luke 3:14; Rom. 13:4; Matt. 8:9–10; Acts 10:1–2; Rev. 17:14, 16).

The office of the magistrate is a lawful calling, and hence a Christian may occupy that station if he has been appropriately called to it. When a Christian holds civil office, certain things are required of him. He is called to maintain piety, justice, and peace. These things are to be defined according to the wholesome laws of the commonwealth in which this magistrate holds office. When the question arises, as it will, by what standard "wholesome laws" are identified, the only answer that can be given is the standard of Scripture. In particular, the Christian magistrate is not prohibited from waging war, even though the New Covenant has now been established among men. But he must only wage war upon just and necessary occasion.

3. The civil magistrate may not assume to himself the administration of the Word and sacraments, or the power of the keys of the kingdom of heaven (2 Chron. 26:18; Matt. 18:17; 16:19; 1 Cor. 12:28–29; Eph. 4:11–12; 1 Cor. 4:1–2; Rom. 10:15; Heb. 5:4): yet he hath authority, and it is his duty, to take order that unity and peace be preserved in the Church, that the truth of God be kept pure and entire, that all blasphemies and heresies be suppressed, all corruptions and abuses in worship and discipline prevented or reformed, and all the ordinances of God duly settled, administered, and observed (Isa. 49:23; Ps. 122:9; Ezra 7:23, 25–28; Lev. 24:16; Deut. 13:5–6, 12; 2 Ki. 18:4; 1 Chron. 13:1–9; 2 Ki. 24:1–16; 2 Chron. 34:33; 15:12–13). For the better effecting whereof, he hath power to call synods, to be present at them and to provide

that whatsoever is transacted in them be according to the mind of God (2 Chron. 19:8–11; 2 Chron. 29; 30; Matt. 2:4–5).

The civil magistrate may not usurp the prerogatives of the Church. He may not discharge the office of preaching the Word, and he may not administer the sacraments. Neither may he conduct or oversee the process of church discipline; he does not have the power of the keys. In our era, this doctrine needs to be strongly reasserted. When someone is excommunicated from the Church, he does not have the right to sue in the civil courts. The fact that this is happening in our era is a resurgence of Erastianism. In short, the magistrate does not have authority *in sacris*.

He does have authority *circa sacra*. If public tumult breaks out in the church, for example, the magistrate must take steps to restore order. He has the responsibility to see that the truth is maintained, that blasphemy and heresy be repressed, idolatry excluded, etc. In brief, the magistrate has authority over false religion. This means that he has an indirect effect on true religion.

As a churchman of eminence, he has the authority to convene a council of the true church, to attend it himself or through representatives, and ensure that the result of the synod is according to the will of God. Although I am in far greater sympathy with the original Westminster Confession at this point than with the American version, this last item is problematic. How can the magistrate be the final arbiter of the deliberations of the synod unless it is a corrupt synod, or unless the magistrate in some sense has been given the ministry of the Word?

The American downgrade of paragraph III (as revised in 1789):

3. Civil magistrates may not assume to themselves the administration of the Word and sacraments (2 Chron. 26:18); or the power of the keys of the kingdom of heaven (Matt. 18:17; 16:19; 1 Cor.

12:28–29; Eph. 4:11–12; 1 Cor. 4:1–2; Rom. 10:15; Heb. 5:4); or, in the least, interfere in matters of faith (John 18:36; Mal. 2:7; Acts 5:29). Yet, as nursing fathers, it is the duty of civil magistrates to protect the Church of our common Lord, without giving the preference to any denomination of Christians above the rest, in such a manner that all ecclesiastical persons whatever shall enjoy the full, free, and unquestioned liberty of discharging every part of their sacred functions, without violence or danger (Isa. 49:23). And, as Jesus Christ hath appointed a regular government and discipline in his Church, no law of any commonwealth should interfere with, let, or hinder, the due exercise thereof, among the voluntary members of any denomination of Christians, according to their own profession and belief (Ps. 105:15; Acts 18:14–15). It is the duty of civil magistrates to protect the person and good name of all their people, in such an effectual manner as that no person be suffered, either upon pretence of religion or of infidelity, to offer any indignity, violence, abuse, or injury to any other person whatsoever: and to take order, that all religious and ecclesiastical assemblies be held without molestation or disturbance (2 Sam. 23:3; 1 Tim. 2:1–2; Rom. 13:4).

We have no difference with this until we come to the statement that the magistrate may not interfere in matter of faith "in the least." That would create interesting problems. As a nursing father, the magistrate is to protect the Christian church, but to do so without giving any preference to any body of Christians above the others. Here the American version grows utterly unwieldy. Define "Christian." The basic question is whether or not the magistrate must be required to be a Christian, and whether or not this has any creedal aspect.

The Confession goes on to say that laws cannot interfere with how people decide to voluntarily join themselves to the church of their choice. The only restriction on religious liberty that the magistrate may offer concerns the bogus right of one worshipper to assault or insult another.

4. It is the duty of people to pray for magistrates (1 Tim. 2:1–2), to honour their persons (1 Pet. 2:17), to pay them tribute or other dues (Rom. 13:6–7), to obey their lawful commands, and to be subject to their authority, for conscience' sake (Rom. 13:5; Titus 3:1). Infidelity, or difference in religion, doth not make void the magistrates' just and legal authority, nor free the people from their due obedience to them (1 Pet. 2:13–14, 16): from which ecclesiastical persons are not exempted (Rom. 13:1; 1 Ki. 2:35; Acts 25:9–11; 2 Pet. 2:1, 10–11; Jude 8–11), much less hath the Pope any power and jurisdiction over them in their dominions, or over any of their people; and, least of all, to deprive them of their dominions, or lives, if he shall judge them to be heretics, or upon any other pretence whatsoever (2 Thess. 2:4; Rev. 13:15–17).

A Christian people have a collection of duties with regard to the magistrate placed over them. They must first pray for them and honor their persons. They must pay taxes as appropriate and obey them when the commands are lawful. They are to defer to the authority of the magistrate, and they are to do this out of conscience, and not from fear. The fact that a magistrate may be a wicked man, or an agnostic, does not remove the authority of the magistrate at all. The people are not freed from their obligation to obey because of the spiritual condition of the magistrate. In this respect, ministers are under authority just like everyone else, and no minister, including the pope, can wield civil authority over the magistrate. We have here the outlines of a doctrine of sphere sovereignty.

CHAPTER 24
Of Marriage and Divorce

On top of everything else, marriage and divorce turn out to be political issues as well. For those who know how to think properly, everything is connected.

> 1. Marriage is to be between one man and one woman: neither is it lawful for any man to have more than one wife, nor for any woman to have more than one husband, at the same time (Gen. 2:24; Matt. 19:5–6; Prov. 2:17).

One man, one woman, one time. Polygamy is excluded because it is not in keeping with God's creation design for man and woman. God created Adam and one woman, not Adam and three women. Christ is the bridegroom of the church, and Christ provides the ultimate example of monogamy. The elders of the Christian church are required to be monogamous, thus reflecting this ultimate pattern. The Old Testament examples of polygamy are not to be categorized as sinful in the same way that adultery is, but polygamy did definitely fall short of the creation pattern, and thus is now unlawful in Christian cultures. Polyandry is excluded in the very nature of things. A husband is the head of his wife, and if a wife has two husbands, she is placed in an impossible governmental situation. A man cannot serve two masters, and neither can a woman.

> 2. Marriage was ordained for the mutual help of husband and wife (Gen. 2:18), for the increase of mankind with a legitimate issue, and of the Church with an holy seed (Mal. 2:15); and for preventing of uncleanness (1 Cor. 7:2, 9).

Why is marriage? First, the husband and wife are created to provide godly help to one another—companionship in the fullest sense of that word. Secondly, God knew that Adam was unable to populate the world by himself, and so He gave him the woman. The purpose of our being constituted male and female is the propagation of godly offspring. And, thirdly, marriage is ordained for the sake of the marriage bed, which in a fallen world is a great help in the prevention of various forms of sexual immorality.

> 3. It is lawful for all sorts of people to marry, who are able with judgment to give their consent (Heb. 13:4; 1 Tim. 4:3; 1 Cor. 7:36–38; Gen. 24:57–58). Yet is it the duty of Christians to marry only in the Lord (1 Cor. 7:39). And therefore such as profess the true reformed religion should not marry with infidels, papists, or other idolaters: neither should such as are godly be unequally yoked, by marrying with such as are notoriously wicked in their life, or maintain damnable heresies (Gen. 34:14; Exod. 34:16; Deut. 7:3–4; 1 Ki. 11:4; Neh. 13:25–27; Mal. 2:11–12; 2 Cor. 6:14).

Just as God gave permission to eat from any of the trees in the Garden of Eden, so men and women may marry as they please, and marry whom they please. One important restriction must be remembered—Christians must only marry Christians. In the first place, this means that those who profess the true reformed religion may not marry those who are overtly outside the pale, such as atheists, papists, or idolaters in other respects. But it is also possible for individuals to profess the true religion, but to live in a wicked way, or to profess heretical opinions. The fact that they externally belong to the same church as a true believer does not make them a lawful candidate for marriage.

> 4. Marriage ought not to be within the degrees of consanguinity or affinity forbidden by the Word (Lev. 18; 1 Cor. 5:1; Amos 2:7). Nor can such incestuous marriages ever be made lawful by any law of man or consent of parties, so as those persons may live together as man and wife (Mark 6:18; Lev. 18:24–28). **The man may not marry any of his wife's kindred, nearer in blood than he may of his own: nor the woman of her husband's kindred, nearer in blood than of her own (Lev. 20:19–21).**

The Old Testament restrictions on marriage continue. A man may not marry his sister, for example. The important thing to note here is that the law of man, or agreement of parties, cannot make such a union into a marriage. In such an instance, we would have to speak of "marriage," just as we do with homosexual "marriages." A brother and sister who got "married," assuming it to have been legal, should, upon repentance, separate and divorce. This would not be the requirement, for example, of someone who married unlawfully in another way (e.g., unlawfully divorced before the marriage). In that situation, repentance would not result in a divorce. The section in bold was dropped by the Presbyterian Church in the United States in 1886, and is not in the PCA version of the Confession, which is a good thing. The restriction there goes beyond the boundaries of Scripture, and, in a certain measure, against Scripture.

> 5. Adultery or fornication committed after a contract, being detected before marriage, giveth just occasion to the innocent party to dissolve that contract (Matt. 1:18–20). In the case of adultery after marriage, it is lawful for the innocent party to sue out a

divorce (Matt. 5:31–32): and, after the divorce, to marry another, as if the offending party were dead (Matt. 19:9; Rom. 7:2–3).

An engagement may be broken if there is infidelity on the part of the other person after the engagement is made. Although the Confession does not address the question, an engagement may also be broken if there was earlier hidden immorality.

Say, for example, that a woman represented herself as a virgin although she was not. If the man enters into the betrothal believing this to be the case, when he discovers the truth, he may break the engagement (or marriage). In the case of adultery, the innocent person may divorce the other and is completely free from the law of marriage in every respect. It is as though the offending party had died, because behavior has consequences.

> 6. Although the corruption of man be such as is apt to study arguments unduly to put asunder those whom God hath joined together in marriage: yet, nothing but adultery, or such willful desertion as can no way be remedied by the Church, or civil magistrate, is cause sufficient of dissolving the bond of marriage (Matt. 19:8–9; 1 Cor. 7:15; Matt. 19:6): wherein, a public and orderly course of proceeding is to be observed; and the persons concerned in it not left to their own wills, and discretion, in their own case (Deut. 24:1–4).

Men like to "study arguments" that might be able to get them into bed with other women. The fact that the Bible allows for divorce under certain conditions should not be used to rationalize or justify lust. But only two conditions may set a person free to marry another. The first is adultery, and has already been addressed. The second is willful desertion that is beyond ecclesiastical or civil remedy. And when the conditions are met, the obtaining of a divorce should be a big deal, with a judicial and open approach being taken, and the aggrieved person not left to adjudicate their own case. In a corrupt time, as ours is, the civil and ecclesiastical authorities will frequently refuse to do their duty. In such a case, the innocent person may have to make their own decisions, but this is not the way it ought to be.

Unit Twelve: For Further Study

Reading Assignments

Hodge, pp. 293–309, 427–429 [Chapters 23–24, Appendix 3]

Turretin, Vol. 2, pp. 165–168 [Eleventh Topic: Question 26] and Vol. 3, pp. 316–336 [Eighteenth Topic: Question 34]

Questions on Reading

1. Does Hodge believe that God has required any particular form of civil government for men?

2. What is the point of civil government?

3. What should a Christian magistrate also seek?

4. May Christian magistrates wage war?

5. What two civil arrangements does Hodge oppose?

6. Is marriage a religious contract only?

7. Does Turretin believe that the laws of the Old Testament are abrogated?

8. According to Turretin, does a believing magistrate have any responsibilities for the church?

9. What kind of right does the magistrate have in sacred things?

10. Can a magistrate compel men to faith?

UNIT THIRTEEN

CHAPTER 25
Of the Church

And so now we come to the doctrine of the Church, simultaneously clear and confusing.

> 1. The catholic or universal Church, which is invisible, consists of the whole number of the elect, that have been, are, or shall be gathered into one, under Christ the Head thereof; and is the spouse, the body, the fullness of Him that filleth all in all (Eph. 1:10, 22–23; 5:23, 27, 32; Col. 1:18).

The invisible catholic Church is defined here as the elect, all the chosen of God from the beginning of the world to the end of it. As the elect, they constitute the body of Christ, His bride. He is the Head of the Church, and the Church (in this sense) is the fullness of Christ, who is in turn the fullness of everything. Thus defined, there is no immediate problem with affirming that the elect are the invisible Church. Some possible downstream problems (depending on applications) will be addressed in the following section.

> 2. The visible Church, which is also catholic or universal under the Gospel (not confined to one nation, as before under the law), consists of all those throughout the world that profess the true

religion (1 Cor. 1:2; 12:12–13; Ps. 2:8; Rev. 7:9; Rom. 15:9–12); and of their children (1 Cor. 7:14; Acts 2:39; Ezek. 16:20–21; Rom. 11:16; Gen. 3:15; 17:7): and is the kingdom of the Lord Jesus Christ (Matt. 13:47; Isa. 9:7), the house and family of God (Eph. 2:19; 3:15), out of which there is no ordinary possibility of salvation (Acts 2:47).

The visible Church is also catholic in an earthly sense, meaning that it is no longer confined to one nation, as it was when it was under the law. This visible Church is composed of anyone in the world who professes (biblically) to believe the Christian faith. When they make this profession, their children are included with them. This visible Church is to be understood as the kingdom of the Lord Jesus. This Church is the household of God, and outside of this Church there is no ordinary possibility of salvation. And outside of the invisible church (in the sense defined above), there is no possibility of salvation whatsoever.

But here is another of those rare places where we must differ with the Confession of Faith, although it is not a difference of substance, but rather a difference in how a metaphor is to be applied. A problem can be created when you affirm a belief in two Churches, one visible and the other invisible. Are they the same Church or not? If they are, then why are "membership rosters" different? If they are not the same, then which one is the true Church? We know that Christ has only one bride. The natural supposition is that the invisible Church, because it is made up of the elect, must be the true Church. But this could tend to a disparagement of the visible Church and eventually necessitates, I believe, a baptistic understanding of the visible Church. Because time and history are not taken into account, we have two Churches, on different ontological levels.

We could make the same point, and it would be less problematic, if we considered the one Church under a different set of terms, and still preserve the necessary distinction made by visible and invisible. Those replacement terms would be *historical* and *eschatological*. Because time and history are taken into account, we preserve the understanding of just one Church, while preserving the necessary distinction between those church members who are finally saved because they were foreordained to that salvation and those who are finally lost. The historical Church is the counterpart to the visible Church and consists of those throughout history who profess the true faith, together with their children. The eschatological Church is the elect, but when it is revealed, it will not be invisible. At the last day, every true child of God will be there, not one missing, and every false professor will have been removed.

A second problem with the Confession here is the assumption that the Jews of the Old Covenant constituted the historical Church, period, outside of which there was no ordinary possibility of salvation. But the nation of Israel was established to be a priestly nation among the nations. Many thousands outside of Israel were saved in the time of the law. What about Melchizedek, Job, Lot, Jethro, Namaan, the inhabitants of Ninevah who repented under the preaching of Jonah, and those Gentile worshippers for whom Solomon prayed at the dedication of the Temple?

> 3. Unto this catholic visible Church Christ hath given the ministry, oracles, and ordinances of God, for the gathering and perfecting of the saints, in this life, to the end of the world: and doth, by His own presence and Spirit, according to His promise, make them effectual thereunto (1 Cor. 12:28; Eph. 4:11–13; Matt. 28:19–20; Isa. 59:21).

Within the visible Church, Christ ministers by various means of His appointment. He has granted the ministry of God to the Church, the oracles of God to the Church, and the ordinances of God to the Church. He has done this so that the saints could be gathered and perfected in the context of His household throughout the course of their lives. This Church will remain until the end of the world, doing this essential work. Christ, through His covenantal presence and through His Spirit, makes all these gifts effectual to their appointed end. The Lord's Supper is effectual because Christ makes it so. The preaching of the Word is effectual because Christ makes it so.

> 4. This catholic Church hath been sometimes more, sometimes less visible (Rom. 11:3–4; Rev. 12:6, 14). And particular Churches, which are members thereof, are more or less pure, according as the doctrine of the Gospel is taught and embraced, ordinances administered, and public worship performed more or less purely in them (Rev. 2; 3; 1 Cor. 5:6–7).

A perfectionistic approach to the visible or historical Church is not biblical. The catholic, visible Church does not always present the same degree of visibility or purity. And particular churches, members of the catholic Church, exhibit this same tendency. They are more or less pure, depending on how the Gospel is taught and embraced, depending on how the ordinances are practiced, and depending on the purity of worship in their service of God. The visible, historic Church is on a dimmer switch, not an on/off switch.

> 5. The purest Churches under heaven are subject both to mixture and error (1 Cor. 13:12; Rev. 2; 3; Matt. 13:24–30, 47); and some have so degenerated, as to become no Churches of Christ, but synagogues of Satan (Rev. 18:2; Rom. 11:18–22). Nevertheless, there shall be always a Church on earth to worship God according to His will (Matt. 16:18; Ps. 72:17; 102:28; Matt. 28:19–20).

No perfect Church exists in this fallen world. All Churches are fallible and are prone to error and compromise. This does not necessarily alter their status as churches of Christ. Left unchecked, however, the mixture and error does threaten their status as churches of Christ eventually because it is possible for a particular church to degenerate to the point where apostasy occurs. In Romans 11, the apostle Paul warns the Gentile churches that they may fall through covenantal presumption in just the same way that the Jews fell. Particular churches can be removed from the olive tree. However the olive tree itself will always stand.

This is why we can say there will always be a Church on earth to worship God according to His will. The olive tree will never be chopped down, and one day she will fill the earth with her fruit. But this does not mean that particular branches cannot be pruned from the tree. This is why we insist that the catholic Church was given a promise that she would never fall. The Church at Rome was given no such promise, and, in fact, the dire covenantal warnings mentioned above (with regard to severance from the olive tree) were delivered expressly *to* the church at Rome. They are found, after all, in the letter to the *Romans*.

> 6. There is no other head of the Church but the Lord Jesus Christ (Col. 1:18; Eph. 1:22). Nor can the Pope of Rome, in any sense, be head thereof: **but is that Antichrist, that man of sin, and son of perdition, that exalteth himself, in the Church, against Christ and all that is called God (Matt. 23:8–10; 2 Thess. 2:3–4, 8–9; Rev. 13:6).**

The Church cannot have an earthly head, but only the Lord Jesus Christ. This particularly excludes the bishop of Rome. The section in bold, identifying the pope as the Antichrist, has been deleted from the American version of the Confession. This improvement involves more than rejecting just an interesting doctrinal understanding of the papacy. This removal opens the way for a preterist understanding of New Testament prophecy, over against this particular historicist understanding. It does not necessarily indicate any particular friendship to the pope to stop calling him the Antichrist.

CHAPTER 26
Of the Communion of Saints

What is the communion of saints, which we confess in the Apostles' Creed?

1. All saints, that are united to Jesus Christ their Head, by His Spirit, and by faith, have fellowship with Him in His grace, sufferings, death, resurrection, and glory (1 John 1:3; Eph. 3:16–19; John 1:16; Eph. 2:5–6; Phil. 3:10; Rom. 6:5–6; 2 Tim. 2:12): and, being united to one another in love, they have communion in each other's gifts and graces (Eph. 4:15–16; 1 Cor. 12:7; 3:21–23; Col. 2:19), and are obliged to the performance of such duties, public and private, as do conduce to their mutual good, both in the inward and outward man (1 Thess. 5:11, 14; Rom. 1:11–12, 14; 1 John 3:16–18; Gal. 6:10).

Referring here to the company of the regenerate (the saints are those united to Christ by the Spirit and by faith), the Westminster theologians make the scriptural point that such regenerate believers have complete fellowship in Christ in all that He has—grace, suffering, etc. As a result of being united to Christ, they are therefore united to one another in love. How could two people both be united to Christ, and not be united to one another? With this union, we are tied together in our gifts and graces. Following this, we are bound in our duties one to another. These duties are both public and private, and pertain to the good of one another, whether external or internal.

> 2. Saints by profession are bound to maintain an holy fellowship and communion in the worship of God, and in performing such other spiritual services as tend to their mutual edification (Heb. 10:24–25; Acts 2:42, 46; Isa. 2:3; 1 Cor. 11:20); as also in relieving each other in outward things, according to their several abilities and necessities. Which communion, as God offereth opportunity, is to be extended unto all those who, in every place, call upon the name of the Lord Jesus (Acts 2:44–45; 2 Cor. 8; 9; 1 John 3:17; Acts 11:29–30).

At the center of our duties to one another, we find our duty to maintain this union in the worship of God. In other words, the point of unity should be cultivated in order to maintain our unity. If we turn to face one another as the principle of unity, we lose our ability to keep the unity. But unity in worship does not exclude ministering to one another in the necessities of this life—food, shelter, comfort, etc. The only requirements for this communion would be the common faith, and the providential opportunities.

> 3. This communion which the saints have with Christ, doth not make them in any wise partakers of the substance of His Godhead; or to be equal with Christ in any respect: either of which to affirm is impious and blasphemous (Col. 1:18–19; 1 Cor. 8:6; Isa. 42:8; 1 Tim. 6:15–16; Ps. 45:7; Heb. 1:8–9). Nor doth their communion one with another, as saints, take away, or infringe the title or propriety which each man hath in his goods and possessions (Exod. 20:15; Eph. 4:28; Acts 5:4).

Our communion with Christ is covenantal, and not ontological. If we neglect covenant theology, we get into trouble because the Bible clearly teaches our union with Him. But if there is no such thing as covenant union, then ontological union is the only option left. In the same way, the saints do not become ontologically one with each other, making property and marital relations common. Rather, we are covenantally one with one another, and this means our obligations are limited and defined by covenant.

CHAPTER 27
Of the Word and Sacraments

Church, communion of saints, Word and sacraments—all these issues obviously go together.

> 1. Sacraments are holy signs and seals of the covenant of grace (Rom. 4:11; Gen. 17:7, 10), immediately instituted by God (Matt 28:19; 1 Cor. 11:23), to represent Christ and His benefits; and to confirm our interest in Him (1 Cor. 10:16; 11:25–26; Gal. 3:27; 17): as also, to put a visible difference between those that belong unto the Church and the rest of the world (Rom. 15:8; Exod. 12:48; Gen. 34:14); and solemnly to engage them to the service of God in Christ, according to His Word (Rom. 6:3–4; 1 Cor. 10:16, 21).

What is a sacrament? A sacrament is a sign, and a sign that seals what it signifies. The sacraments of the Christian religion therefore are those which signify and seal the covenant of grace. We know that a practice is such a sacrament if it was instituted by God in order to represent Christ and His salvation. A sacrament is placed upon a particular individual in order to establish a link between the promises of the covenant and that person. A sacrament is also given as a means of distinguishing the saints of God from those who are not. As a result, those with such a divine mark are obligated by it. We must remember in this discussion that sacraments are inescapable; if we do not accept the two sacraments established in the Word of God, then we will make up our own sacraments. Here, sign this card. Throw your pinecone or stick in the fire.

> 2. There is, in every sacrament, a spiritual relation, or sacramental union, between the sign and the thing signified: whence it comes to pass, that the names and effects of the one are attributed to the other (Gen. 17:10; Matt. 26:27–28; Titus 3:5).

This is something we understand quite well in other realms, and it is not hard to master. "With this ring, I thee wed." Really? Metal makes you married? The water cleanses us and washes our sins away. But only a spiritual bonehead would think that water all by itself can wash away sins.

> 3. The grace which is exhibited in or by the sacraments rightly used, is not conferred by any power in them; neither doth the efficacy of a sacrament depend upon the piety or intention of him that doth administer it (Rom. 2:28–29; 1 Pet. 3:21): but upon the work of the Spirit (Matt. 3:11; 1 Cor. 12:13), and the word of institution, which contains, together with a precept authorizing the use thereof, a promise of benefit to worthy receivers (Matt. 26:27–28; 28:19–20).

The sacrament itself has no power; there is power in that which the sacrament is tied to—the blessings and curses of the covenant itself. This being the case, the sacrament does not depend for its efficacy on the godliness of the one administering the sacrament. Suppose a pastor runs off with the church organist the day after somebody's baptism. Does that nullify the baptism? Not at all. The applications of the sacraments are *objective*, meaning that the Spirit is at work in the words of institution. This is what brings about the resultant blessings (or curses).

4. There be only two sacraments ordained by Christ our Lord in the Gospel; that is to say, Baptism, and the Supper of the Lord: neither of which may be dispensed by any, but by a minister of the Word lawfully ordained (Matt. 28:19; 1 Cor. 11:20, 23; 4:1; Heb. 5:4).

As opposed to the teaching of Rome, there are only two sacraments, and not seven: baptism and the Lord's Supper. According to the Confession, they are to be administered by lawfully ordained ministers of the Word. This is a good idea for reasons of good government and accountability, but it should not be a confessional issue. What should be a confessional issue is that the rulers of the Church are responsible to see to it that a right understanding of the sacraments is to be preserved, and so, at the very least, they should oversee and approve all occasions where the sacraments are administered.

5. The sacraments of the old testament, in regard of the spiritual things thereby signified and exhibited, were, for substance, the same with those of the new (1 Cor. 10:1–4).

The New Testament era did not usher in new sacramental realities—the people of God have always had the sacramental reality of initiation and nurture. What changed was the visible nature of the signs, not the constant reality of the things signified.

Unit Thirteen: For Further Study

 Reading Assignments

Hodge, pp. 310–337, 399–419 [Chapters 25–27]

Vincent, pp. 233–234, 241–246 [Chapters 88, 91–93]

Turretin, Vol. 3, pp. 337–342, 361–374 [Nineteenth Topic: Question 1, 8–9]

 Questions on Reading

1. According to Hodge, who must acknowledge that the invisible Church is complete and full?

2. What kind of matter is the relative purity of the visible Church?

3. If Christ has appointed the pope or national sovereigns as heads over the Church, then what is disobedience to their authority? If He has not, then what is their claim?

4. How is union in the communion of saints accomplished?

5. According to Vincent, why are the ordinances called the "ordinary means" for communicating the benefits of salvation to us?

6. How are the sacraments effectual means of salvation in a positive sense?

7. What is signified by the outward sensible signs?

8. According to Turretin, what is the "twofold" matter of a sacrament?

9. What is the "accidental end" of a certain use of the sacraments?

10. What is the sin of "defect" in understanding the sacraments?

UNIT FOURTEEN

CHAPTER 28
Of Baptism

We have addressed the sacraments generally; now it is time for some specifics.

> 1. Baptism is a sacrament of the new testament, ordained by Jesus Christ (Matt. 28:19), not only for the solemn admission of the party baptized into the visible Church (1 Cor. 12:13); but also to be unto him a sign and seal of the covenant of grace (Rom. 4:11; Col. 2:11–12), of his ingrafting into Christ (Gal. 3:27; Rom. 6:5), of regeneration (Titus 3:5), of remission of sins (Mark 1:4), and of his giving up unto God, through Jesus Christ, to walk in the newness of life (Rom. 6:3–4). Which sacrament is, by Christ's own appointment, to be continued in His Church until the end of the world (Matt. 28:19–20).

Here we discuss the two sacraments specifically, in turn. Baptism is one of the sacraments of the new covenant. It was ordained by Jesus Christ as a sacrament in the words of the Great Commission. He told His disciples that the mark of His disciples was to be baptism. Disciple the nations, He said, *baptizing* them. The signification of baptism is twofold, that is, it points in two directions. The first is the solemn recognition that the one baptized has been admitted into the visible Church of Christ. At the same time, baptism also points away from the person, to the objective meanings of baptism. Baptism means the one baptized has a sign and seal of the covenant of grace and has been grafted into Christ; it signifies regeneration, forgiveness of sins, and the obligation to walk in newness of life. This sacrament is perpetual in history.

The two "meanings" of baptism which are not assigned here to the one baptized are regeneration and forgiveness. Baptism means these things, but there is a difference between saying baptism means regeneration and baptism means *my* regeneration. It does not *automatically* mean these things. At the same time, it is *intended* to mean them. It is "to be unto him a sign and seal ... of regeneration."

> 2. The outward element to be used in this sacrament is water, wherewith the party is to be baptized, in the name of the Father, and of the Son, and of the Holy Ghost, by a minister of the Gospel, lawfully called thereunto (Matt. 3:11; John 1:33; Matt. 28:19–20).

The essence of water baptism is found in the application of water to an individual in the name of the Father, Son, and Holy Spirit. This should be done by a minister of the gospel, lawfully ordained. As discussed in the last chapter, this last requirement is perhaps too strict. The minister and elders are responsible for all the baptisms, and consequently, should oversee them, and ordinarily perform them, but this is not essential to the validity of the ordinance. In other words, if someone was baptized in the name of the Father, Son, and Holy Spirit by an orthodox layman, rebaptism would not be necessary. Irregular baptisms are not the same thing as non-baptisms.

> 3. Dipping of the person into the water is not necessary; but Baptism is rightly administered by pouring, or sprinkling water upon the person (Heb. 9:10, 19–22; Acts 2:41; 16:33; Mark 7:4).

Dipping or immersion is certainly permitted, but scripturally it cannot be insisted upon. Baptism is also administered correctly when the water is poured or sprinkled upon the person. Ironically, for many Baptists this is the place where they should begin rethinking their views of baptism. The notion is that "*baptizo* means immersion and nothing else" is very widespread, and it really cannot be defended. Consequently, when Baptists have this demonstrated to them, it may bring about a new openness when talking about the subjects of baptism.

> 4. Not only those that do actually profess faith in and obedience unto Christ (Mark 16:15–16; Acts 8:37–38), but also the infants of one, or both, believing parents, are to be baptized (Gen. 17:7, 9; Gal. 3:9, 14; Col. 2:11–12; Acts 2:38–39; Rom. 4:11–12; 1 Cor. 7:14; Matt. 28:19; Mark 10:13–16; Luke 18:15).

No disagreement exists over the propriety of baptizing pagans upon their profession of faith in Christ, along with their expressed willingness to follow and obey Him. But in addition to this, not only such people should be baptized, but also the infants (or dependent children) of such converts are to be baptized. This is the case even where only one of the parents is converted.

> 5. Although it be a great sin to contemn or neglect this ordinance (Luke 7:30; Exod. 4:24–26), yet grace and salvation are not so inseparably annexed unto it, as that no person can be regenerated, or saved, without it (Rom. 4:11; Acts 10:2, 4, 22, 31, 45, 47): or, that all that are baptized are undoubtedly regenerated (Acts 8:13, 23).

Neglect of baptism is a great sin, but not an unforgivable sin. We are to consider baptism and regeneration together, but we are not to treat this as an absolute. In other words, some who are not baptized will be saved, and not all who are baptized are saved. But the ordinary pattern is to see the two together.

6. The efficacy of Baptism is not tied to that moment of time wherein it is administered (John 3:5, 8); yet, notwithstanding, by the right use of this ordinance, the grace promised is not only offered, but really exhibited, and conferred, by the Holy Ghost, to such (whether of age or infants) as that grace belongeth unto, according to the counsel of God's own will, in His appointed time (Gal. 3:27; Titus 3:5; Eph. 5:25–26; Acts 2:38, 41).

Baptism is efficacious. But the efficacy of the sacrament is *not* tied to the moment when it is administered. This efficacious grace is conferred on the elect at the appropriate time, the time of their conversion, and what happens in that moment is the applied grace of their baptism. For someone baptized in infancy in a covenant home, and who was converted as an adult, the Confession teaches that their conversion was due to the efficacy of their baptism. When someone under such circumstances is not converted, we obviously cannot speak of the saving efficacy of their baptism. But when such a person is converted, it is beyond all question that the Confession teaches that their baptism was *efficacious*, taking the grace promised in baptism, and "really exhibiting and conferring" it. It is common for many contemporary Presbyterians to depart from the Confession here by saying that the two sacraments are genuine means of grace, but that they are means of sanctifying grace only, and not saving grace. This is out of conformity with the Confession at this point—it is not heresy, but it is plainly out of conformity with the Confession, and those who hold to this position need to take an exception to the Confession. We may summarize this section as saying that "the Holy Ghost uses as His instrument a right use of the ordinance of baptism to really exhibit and confer the saving grace promised in that baptism to those elect who are the rightful beneficiaries of that grace."

7. The sacrament of Baptism is but once to be administered unto any person (Titus 3:5).

This being the case, baptism is not to be administered over and over. If it were only efficacious based on the timing of it, then it would have to be administered over and over. But fortunately, it is not. To administer baptism again is therefore to deny that the first baptism was Christian baptism.

CHAPTER 29
Of the Lord's Supper

Baptism is the sign of entry. The Supper is the sacrament of communion and nourishment for those who have entered.

> 1. Our Lord Jesus, in the night wherein He was betrayed, instituted the sacrament of His body and blood, called the Lord's Supper, to be observed in His Church, unto the end of the world, for the perpetual remembrance of the sacrifice of Himself in His death; the sealing all benefits thereof unto true believers, their spiritual nourishment and growth in Him, their further engagement in and to all duties which they owe unto Him; and, to be a bond and pledge of their communion with Him, and with each other, as members of His mystical body (1 Cor. 11:23–26; 10:16–17, 21; 12:13).

The Lord Jesus established this sacrament the night He was betrayed, and the sacrament is very rich in meaning. It is to be commemorated in the Church until the end of the world. For most evangelicals, the meaning of the Supper is limited to the first one mentioned here—and while the understanding is accurate, as far as it goes, it does not go very far. But the import of the Supper goes far beyond a mere memorial. It means the following:

1. A memorial of Christ's self-sacrifice;

2. A sealing of all the benefits of Christ's death unto true believers;

3. A spiritual nourishment of all true believers who partake;

4. A covenant renewal on the part of those who partake;

5. A bond from Him of the fact that He is our God and we are His people;

6. A communion with our fellow believers, fellow members of the body of Christ.

Far more is involved than mere remembering.

> 2. In this sacrament, Christ is not offered up to His Father; nor any real sacrifice made at all, for remission of sins of the quick or dead (Heb. 9:22, 25–26, 28); but only a commemoration of that one offering up of Himself, by Himself, upon the cross, once for all: and a spiritual oblation of all possible praise unto God, for the same (1 Cor. 11:24–26; Matt. 26:26–27): so that the popish sacrifice of the mass (as they call it) is most abominably injurious to Christ's one, only sacrifice, the alone propitiation for all the sins of His elect (Heb. 7:23–24, 27; 10:11–12, 14, 18).

As far as the issue of sacrifice is concerned, the Supper is no real sacrifice, but only a commemoration of a sacrament. But to say it is a commemoration sacrificially does not mean that it is *only* a commemoration in other respects. Christ is not sacrificed to the Father in the Supper. The Supper does involve "all possible praise" for the sacrifice Christ offered, but this is not the same as a sacrifice. The doctrine of the perpetual sacrifice in the Mass is therefore injurious and insulting to the once for all death of Christ on the cross for sins. So the Table is not a sacrifice proper, but it is a sealing "proper," nourishment "proper," covenant renewal "proper," a bond or pact "proper, and a communion with all other saints "proper." In other words it is a false inference to say that because the Supper is not "really" a sacrifice, then it is not "really" anything.

3. The Lord Jesus hath, in this ordinance, appointed His ministers to declare His word of institution to the people; to pray, and bless the elements of bread and wine, and thereby to set them apart from a common to an holy use; and to take and break the bread, to take the cup, and (they communicating also themselves) to give both to the communicants (Matt. 26:26–28; Mark 14:22–24; Luke 22:19–20; 1 Cor. 11:23–26); but to none who are not then present in the congregation (Acts 20:7; 1 Cor. 11:20).

What are the constituent elements of the Supper? What does it take for the Supper to be held?

1. The minister needs to declare the words of institution, showing his authorization to hold the Supper;

2. He should pray;

3. He should bless the bread and wine so that they are sanctified, set apart for this use;

4. He should break the bread;

5. He should take the cup;

6. He should distribute both to the communicants;

7. And his distribution should be limited to those who are present.

This is *what* the supper is, but *where* is it?

4. Private masses, or receiving this sacrament by a priest, or any other, alone (1 Cor. 10:6); as likewise, the denial of the cup to the people (Mark 14:23; 1 Cor. 11:25–29), worshipping the elements, the lifting them up, or carrying them about, for adoration, and the reserving them for any pretended religious use; are all contrary to the nature of this sacrament, and to the institution of Christ (Matt. 15:9).

Distortions of the Supper include these features: private communion, denial of the cup, worshipping the elements, acting in such a way as to provoke such worship, and setting them aside for other religious use.

> 5. The outward elements in this sacrament, duly set apart to the uses ordained by Christ, have such relation to Him crucified, as that, truly, yet sacramentally only, they are sometimes called by the name of the things they represent, to wit, the body and blood of Christ (Matt. 26:26–28); albeit, in substance and nature, they still remain truly and only bread and wine, as they were before (1 Cor. 11:26–28; Matt. 26:29).

The outward elements are not transformed in their nature by any act of consecration. They truly become the body and blood of Christ sacramentally, not physically. The elements remain bread and wine.

> 6. That doctrine which maintains a change of the substance of bread and wine, into the substance of Christ's body and blood (commonly called transubstantiation) by consecration of a priest, or by any other way, is repugnant, not to Scripture alone, but even to common sense, and reason; overthroweth the nature of the sacrament, and hath been, and is, the cause of manifold superstitions; yea, of gross idolatries (Acts 3:21; 1 Cor 11:24–26; Luke 24:6, 39).

The doctrine of transubstantiation is contrary to Scripture. Not only so, but it is also contrary to common sense and reason. It maketh no sense. The error is not a trivial one, because it overthrows the sacrament, and provokes the people into superstition and idolatry.

> 7. Worthy receivers, outwardly partaking of the visible elements, in this sacrament (1 Cor. 11:28), do then also, inwardly by faith, really and indeed, yet not carnally and corporally but spiritually, receive and feed upon, Christ crucified, and all benefits of His death: the body and blood of Christ being then, not corporally or carnally, in, with, or under the bread and wine; yet, as really, but

spiritually, present to the faith of believers in that ordinance, as the elements themselves are to their outward senses (1 Cor. 10:16).

Those who partake of the sacrament really feed upon Christ. But in order to truly feed upon Christ, it is not necessary for the bread and wine to be changed. We feed upon Christ by faith (which is not the same as saying we *pretend* to feed upon Him). We feed spiritually through the bread and wine presented to our outward senses. Christ is presented to us in the sacrament. We see Him there by faith, not by sight. Christ presents Himself to the faith of believers in the same manner that the physical elements present themselves to our hands and mouths.

> 8. Although ignorant and wicked men receive the outward elements in this sacrament; yet, they receive not the thing signified thereby; but, by their unworthy coming thereunto, are guilty of the body and blood of the Lord, to their own damnation. Wherefore, all ignorant and ungodly persons, as they are unfit to enjoy communion with Him, so are they unworthy of the Lord's table; and cannot, without great sin against Christ, while they remain such, partake of these holy mysteries (1 Cor. 11:27–29; 2 Cor. 6:14–16), or be admitted thereunto (1 Cor. 5:6–7, 13; 2 Thess. 3:6, 14–15; Matt. 7:6).

According to the Confession, two types of men should be kept from the Supper—the ignorant and the wicked. When they partake, they do not receive what is signified. If this means that they do not receive the *blessing* promised to any right use of the Supper, then this is correct. But if it means that the wicked do not partake of Christ in *any* respect when they partake of the Supper, then I think this interpretation of the Confession is wrong. The curses of the covenant fall upon wicked and ignorant partakers precisely *because* they defile the body and blood of the Lord. The reason they are guilty of the body and blood of the Lord, as it says here, is because they came to it in an unworthy way. When this happens, they eat and drink to their own damnation. They cannot defile what they did not receive. The contrast at the Table is blessings and curses, not blessings and no blessings.

With regard to the "ignorant," we also want to be careful how we fence the Table here. There are types and degrees of ignorance. For example, there are ignorant people who ought not to be, and so they should be excluded from the Table because their ignorance is culpable. But a five-year-old is necessarily ignorant, and to some extent, so is a mature Christian. We are all *ignorati*, but the Supper is given to nourish and strengthen us (see above). Consequently, we do not want to be maneuvered into saying that Christians should grow big and strong, and then we will give them some food. This aspect of the Confession has to be carefully considered when discussing the issue of child communion, although I do not believe it excludes child communion necessarily. It seems clear that the ignorance addressed by these words is a culpable and stiff-necked ignorance, and not the kind of ignorance which every worthy partaker of the Supper confesses daily.

CHAPTER 30
Of Church Censures

A church without discipline is a church with AIDS—and has no way of fighting off infections.

> 1. The Lord Jesus, as King and Head of His Church, hath therein appointed a government, in the hand of Church officers, distinct from the civil magistrate (Isa. 9:6–7; 1 Tim. 5:17; 1 Thess. 5:12; Acts 20:17–18; Heb. 13:7, 17, 24; 1 Cor. 12:28; Matt. 28:18–20).

The Lord Jesus is the Head of the Church, and the only Head of the Church. As the Head, He has appointed a government in his Church, in the hand of certain officers of the Church. This government is distinct from that of the civil magistrate, and is in no way dependent upon it. We have here a doctrine of sphere sovereignty, and we also see that this means that no earthly form of government is absolute. We see a different kind of check and balance.

> 2. To these officers the keys of the kingdom of heaven are committed; by virtue whereof, they have power, respectively, to retain, and remit sins; to shut that kingdom against the impenitent, both by the Word, and censures; and to open it unto penitent sinners, by the ministry of the Gospel; and by absolution from censures, as occasion shall require (Matt. 16:19; 18:17–18; John 20:21–23; 2 Cor. 2:6–8).

The keys of the kingdom are bestowed upon these officers; in this respect, they are successors of the apostles. What does it mean to have the keys of the kingdom? This is the power to retain and remit sins, and to exclude the unrepentant from the kingdom. This is done both by Word and censure, Word and discipline, administered to those who are within the kingdom, and through the authoritative preaching of the Gospel to repentant sinners who have not yet been brought into the kingdom. The third means is the revocation of an applied censure when the circumstances may warrant.

The ministry of the Word of course includes admonition and rebuke, but must include positive, preventative doctrine as well.

> 3. Church censures are necessary, for the reclaiming and gaining of offending brethren, for deterring of others from the like offenses, for purging out of that leaven which might infect the whole lump, for vindicating the honor of Christ, and the holy profession of the Gospel, and for preventing the wrath of God, which might justly fall upon the Church, if they should suffer His covenant, and the seals thereof, to be profaned by notorious and obstinate offenders (1 Cor. 5; 1 Tim. 5:20; Matt. 7:6; 1 Tim. 1:20; 1 Cor. 11:27–34; Jude 23).

Church censure, or what we call church discipline, is necessary in order to accomplish particular ends. The purposes given are not listed in the order of importance. The point of discipline, first, is to reclaim the erring brother. The second point is so that others will stand in fear, thinking twice before they run off with someone else's wife. Third, the sin if tolerated would threaten to spread and bring the whole church into moral danger. Fourth, Christ is insulted publicly when His people sin, and discipline vindicates His honor. Fifth, the Gospel is insulted when the Church allows members to declare that it does not transform lives. Sixth, the Church acts in self-interest whenever it distances itself from those who are inviting the wrath of God upon them. If the Church permits the covenant and its seals to be profaned by notorious and obstinate offenders, the Church runs a grave risk.

> 4. For the better attaining of these ends, the officers of the Church are to proceed by admonition, suspension from the sacrament of the Lord's Supper for a season; and by excommunication from the Church, according to the nature of the crime, and demerit of the person (1 Thess. 5:12; 2 Thess. 3:6, 14–15; 1 Cor. 5:4–5, 13; Matt. 18:17; Titus 3:10).

The Confession acknowledges three levels of formal censure: The first is admonition, or particular warning, the second is suspension from the Lord's Supper for a period of time, and the last is excommunication. The elders of the Church make the determination on which to apply according to the nature of the crime, and the fault of the individual involved.

CHAPTER 31
Of Synods and Councils

What about the broader church, the church outside the local congregation?

> 1. For the better government, and further edification of the Church, there ought to be such assemblies as are commonly called Synods or Councils (Acts 15:2, 4, 6).

The church has an authoritative presence beyond the local assembly. In this chapter of the Confession we come to the doctrine which separates presbyterianism from the independency which is so common in our era.

> 1. For the better government, and further edification of the Church, there ought to be such assemblies as are commonly called Synods or Councils (Acts 15:2,4,6): and it belongeth to the overseers and other rulers of the particular churches, by virtue of their office, and the power which Christ hath given them for edification and not for destruction, to appoint such assemblies (Acts 15); and to convene together in them, as often as they shall judge it expedient for the good of the Church (Acts 15:22–23, 25). [American Version of paragraph 1, 1789]

Sadly, most of the changes in the American version of the Westminster Confession were not really improvements. This is one of the exceptions. The paragraph makes it clear how the synods are to be constituted and shaped. In short, the councils and synods are not appointed from the top, but are constituted in a "bottom up" representative fashion. It belongs to the bishops and rulers of the local church to appoint such broader assemblies. They are not established, for example, in the same way that the Westminster Assembly was established. No set time is established for how frequently they meet; this is not a confessional issue, but rather one determined by the conditions of the church at the time.

> **2. As magistrates may lawfully call a synod of ministers, and other fit persons, to consult and advise with, about matters of religion (Isa. 49:23; 1 Tim. 2:1–2; 2 Chron. 19:8–11; 29:1–36; 30:1–27; Mal. 2:4–5; Prov. 11:14); so, if magistrates be open enemies to the Church, the ministers of Christ, of themselves, by virtue of their office, or they, with other fit persons upon delegation from their Churches, may meet together in such assemblies (Acts 15:2, 4, 22–23, 25).** [This paragraph deleted in the American version, and subsequent paragraphs renumbered.]

In the older view of Christendom, a Christian magistrate had the power to convene a lawful assembly of the Church. He could not tell them what to say, but he could tell them that they had to say something. He had authority *circa sacra*, but not *in sacris*. He could convene this assembly of the Church from the number of her ministers, as well as other fit individuals—theologians and such. Of course, if the magistrates were hostile to the faith, then ministers could convene an assembly themselves or be sent by the particular churches, along with other fit persons, to meet in such a synod.

3. It belongeth to synods and councils, ministerially to determine controversies of faith, and cases of conscience; to set down rules and directions for better ordering of the public worship of God, and government of His Church; to receive complaints in cases of maladministration, and to authoritatively to determine the same: which decrees and determinations, if consonant to the Word of God, are to be received with reverence and submission; not only for their agreement with the Word, but also for the power whereby they are made, as being an ordinance of God appointed thereunto in His Word (Acts 15:15, 19, 24, 27–31; 16:4; Matt. 18:17–20).

So what does a synod *do*? They determine controversies surrounding the faith, as well as cases of conscience. They establish the order of worship for the churches, as well as the government of the churches. They handle complaints about poor administration in particular churches, and settle the complaints authoritatively. If their decrees accord with the Word of God, they are to be received with reverence and submission on two counts: The first is the agreement with the Word, and the second is the authority they have had assigned to them as a governing body in the Word. The implication of the Confession here is that a local church can disregard a synod if its decision is not in accordance with the Word.

4. All synods or councils, since the Apostles' times, whether general or particular, may err; and many have erred. Therefore they are not to be made the rule of faith, or practice; but to be used as a help in both (Eph. 2:20; Acts 17:11; 1 Cor. 2:5; 2 Cor. 1:24).

Synods and councils of all kinds are not infallible. Consequently they are not to be made the rule of faith or practice, but as an aid to faith and an aid to practice. The word of the Church is authoritative, but not normative. It should be noted that this paragraph of the

Westminster Confession applies to the Westminster Assembly, as the men there knew that it did.

> 5. Synods and councils are to handle, or conclude nothing, but that which is ecclesiastical: and are not to intermeddle with civil affairs which concern the commonwealth, unless by way of humble petition in cases extraordinary; or, by way of advice, for satisfaction of conscience, if they be thereunto required by the civil magistrate (Luke 12:13–14; John 18:36).

Ministers in synod are not to stray from their assigned sphere. They are not to meddle in partisan politics unless the situation is extraordinary, and even then they are to remember their place and only express themselves in great humility. If the magistrate asks advice, with regard to his conscience, they may give it. But here, the advice is only advice.

CHAPTER 32
Of the State of Men After Death,
and of the Resurrection of the Dead

We believe in the resurrection of the dead.

1. The bodies of men, after death, return to dust, and see corruption (Gen. 3:19; Acts 13:36): but their souls, which neither die nor sleep, having an immortal subsistence, immediately return to God who gave them (Luke 23:43; Eccl. 12:7): the souls of the righteous, being then made perfect in holiness, are received into the highest heavens, where they behold the face of God, in light and glory, waiting for the full redemption of their bodies (Heb. 12:23; 2 Cor. 5:1, 6, 8; Phil. 1:23; Acts 3:21; Eph. 4:10). And the souls of the wicked are cast into hell, where they remain in torments and utter darkness, reserved to the judgment of the great day (Luke 16:23–24; Acts 1:25; Jude 6–7; 1 Pet. 3:19). Beside these two places, for souls separated from their bodies, the Scripture acknowledgeth none.

Our bodies are corruptible, and when we die, they disintegrate and return to dust. But our souls do not die (and do not literally sleep) because of the nature of the case. This does not mean our souls are *essentially* immortal, but only that they do not partake of the same corruptions as our bodies. Our souls are immortal in fact (because they do not die), but this does not mean that our souls are not contingent and creaturely. When we die, our souls return to God. The righteous go to be with God immediately, while waiting for the final resurrection of the body. The souls of the unrighteous are cast into hell, according to the Confession, where they undergo torment and utter darkness while they wait for the final judgment. The Confession says that besides heaven and hell, the Scripture does not acknowledge any other place, which I think is overstated. In the interests of combating Roman Catholic merit-mongering, and the unbiblical doctrine of Purgatory, the Westminster fathers here fell short of what Scripture actually teaches. *Hades* or *Sheol* is not the same as *Gehenna*, and it is a place for departed spirits. Prior to the resurrection of Christ, Hades also contained Paradise, or the bosom of Abraham. This does not lend any credence to the Romanist views of purgation, but the existence of more than two places should still be acknowledged. The Church should at some time revise the Confession here to say that there are no more than two *final* or *ultimate* destinations and use different wording to exclude the doctrine of Purgatory.

> 2. At the last day, such as are found alive shall not die, but be changed (1 Thess. 4:17; 1 Cor. 15:51–52): and all the dead shall be raised up, with the self-same bodies, and none other (although with different qualities), which shall be united again to their souls forever (Job 19:26–27; 1 Cor. 15:42–44).

On the day of resurrection, the people who are alive at that time will be transformed. The dead will be raised, and the bodies they will receive will be the same bodies that went into the ground. This does not mean there are no changes, but it does mean that there is a fundamental continuity. Once the reunion of soul and body is accomplished, they will never again be separated.

3. The bodies of the unjust shall, by the power of Christ, be raised to dishonour: the bodies of the just, by His Spirit, unto honour; and be made conformable to His own glorious body (Acts 24:15; John 5:28–29; 1 Cor. 15:43; Phil. 3:21).

There is a resurrection of the unjust as well. They will be raised to dishonor. The just will be raised to honor, that honor meaning a thorough conformity to the body of Christ.

CHAPTER 33
Of the Last Judgment

The final things belong to the Lord our God.

> 1. God hath appointed a day, wherein He will judge the world, in righteousness, by Jesus Christ (Acts 17:31), to whom all power and judgment is given of the Father (John 5:22, 27). In which day, not only the apostate angels shall be judged (1 Cor. 6:3; Jude 6; 2 Pet. 2:4), but likewise all persons that have lived upon earth shall appear before the tribunal of Christ, to give an account of their thoughts, words, and deeds; and to receive according to what they have done in the body, whether good or evil (2 Cor. 5:10; Eccl. 12:14; Rom. 2:16; 14:10, 12; Matt. 12:36–37).

The world will be judged on an appointed day, appointed by God. The judgment will be entirely righteous, and meted out by the Lord Jesus Christ. In this great day of assembly, all the angels will be judged, as well as every man who ever lived. They will be called to give an account for all their thoughts, words, and deeds.

> 2. The end of God's appointing this day is for the manifestation of the glory of His mercy, in the eternal salvation of the elect; and of His justice, in the damnation of the reprobate, who are wicked and disobedient. For then shall the righteous go into everlasting

life, and receive that fullness of joy and refreshing, which shall come from the presence of the Lord: but the wicked who know not God, and obey not the Gospel of Jesus Christ, shall be cast into eternal torments, and be punished with everlasting destruction from the presence of the Lord, and from the glory of His power (Matt. 25:31–46; Rom. 2:5–6; Rom. 9:22–23; Matt. 25:21; Acts 3:19; 2 Thess. 1:7–10).

This day of judgment is the great display case of two of God's attributes which would otherwise have gone unrecognized. Those two attributes are, respectively, His mercy to the elect, and His justice, which falls upon the reprobate. The elect will enter into everlasting life, and the lost will descend into eternal torments. The saved will be blessed in the presence of the Lord, while the lost will be shut out (covenantally) from the presence of the Lord.

3. As Christ would have us to be certainly persuaded that there shall be a day of judgment, both to deter all men from sin; and for the greater consolation of the godly in their adversity (2 Pet. 3:11, 14; 2 Cor. 5:10–11; 2 Thess. 1:5–7; Luke 21:7, 28; Rom. 8:23–25): so will He have that day unknown to men, that they may shake off all carnal security, and be always watchful, because they know not at what hour the Lord will come; and may be ever prepared to say, Come Lord Jesus, come quickly. Amen (Matt. 24:36, 42–44; Mark 13:35–37; Luke 12:35–36; Rev. 22:20).

Christ wants us to know two things about the great day of judgment. The first truth is that the day is fixed and coming. This deters men from sin, and it comforts the godly who must undergo adversity. But God also wants the name of the day to be unknown so that men will not drift into carnal reasoning about it—saying for example, that they will repent in time for the predicted day of judgment. We must live as though the day could be at any time.

Unit Fourteen: For Further Study

 ## Reading Assignments

Hodge, pp. 338–397 [Chapters 28–33]

Vincent, pp. 246–266, 102–109 [Questions 94–97, 37–39]

Turretin, Vol. 3, pp. 410–428, 293–316 [Nineteenth Topic: Questions 19–21; Eighteenth Topic: Questions 32–33]

Questions on Reading

1. According to Hodge, what kind of action is the action of baptism?

2. Were infants members of the church in the older covenant?

3. What kind of kingdom is the church?

4. Who will be present at the last day of judgment?

5. According to Vincent, what does the water of baptism signify?

6. Why does Vincent think the inclusion of infants in the Old Testament was never taken away or removed?

7. Where do Christians go when they die?

8. According to Turretin, how are infants included in the Great Commission?

9. What word is used to describe the sacrament of the Supper most frequently?

10. What is the first reason for church discipline?

APPENDIX
Answers to Questions on Reading

Unit One

1. According to Hodge, to what extent can "Creeds and Confessions" bind the consciences of men?

    Only to the extent they are scriptural (p. 3).

2. What are the limits placed on the Church when it comes to making conditions of membership?

    The Church may not create conditions for membership that God has not made conditional for salvation (p. 3).

3. What is Hodge's argument for the canonical list for Old Testament books as received by Protestants?

    He argues that the Protestant Old Testament is identical to the Scriptures that were received as such by Jesus and the apostles (pp. 31–32).

4. What is the first argument that Vincent appeals to in showing that the Scriptures are the Word of God?

    His first argument is from the majesty of the Scriptures (p. 17).

5. What is the difference in how Christ is revealed in the Old and the New Testaments?

    In the New Testament He is revealed "without types and figures" (p. 21).

6. What would make the Church an infallible authority, according to Vincent?

    If the authority of Scripture were dependent upon the Church (p. 22).

7. What love must we have in reading and hearing the Scriptures?

    We must love the Word because it is the Word of God (p. 240).

8. According to Turretin, does the Old Testament still serve as a canon of faith and rule of practice?

    Yes, he argues this against the Anabaptists (p. 98). The Old Testament, no less than the New, pertains to Christians.

9. For Turretin, what are the touchstone languages for interpreting Scripture?

    Hebrew in the Old Testament, and Greek in the New (p. 114).

10. Did Turretin hold that the Septuagint was authentic?

    No, he denied that (p. 127), while valuing it highly among translations, or what he calls "versions."

Unit Two

1. According to Hodge, what relation does God as "personal spirit" have to the world?

    He is distinct from it (p. 48).

2. In what way does Scripture condescend to our weakness in talking about God?

    Scripture speaks metaphorically, as though God had a body like ours (p. 49).

3. What does Hodge say about the nature of the one God?

    He says that Father, Son, and Holy Ghost are each equally the one God (p. 57).

4. What distinction does he make between attributes and properties?

    Attributes are the characteristics of the divine essence and therefore common to each of the three persons. Properties are peculiar to each of the persons (pp. 59–60).

5. According to Vincent, what is the wisdom of God?

    It is an essential property, whereby, by one simple and eternal act, He knows both Himself and all possible things perfectly (p. 29).

6. Does Vincent think God can do absolutely anything?

    Anything that does not violate His own nature and character. He can do anything that does not imply contradiction or necessitate imperfection (p. 31).

7. Does Vincent say that the essence of God is the same in all three persons?

    Yes (p. 38).

8. According to Turretin, where does the infinity of God "reside"?

    It is diffused throughout all His attributes (p. 194).

9. For Turretin, do we have adequate vocabulary for talking about the ubiquity of God?

    No (p. 197), and we must therefore borrow terminology from finite, physical things.

10. In what sense is the Trinity a fundamental article, and in what sense not?

    It is necessary to affirm that God is triune, but not necessary to understand the wherefores or hows (p. 263).

Unit Three

1. According to Hodge, do the decrees of God include the sinful actions of men?

    Yes, they do (p. 65).

2. Which groups did not think that God could foresee the future actions of men?

    The Socinians and Rationalists (p.66).

3. What group does Hodge say grants the foreknowledge of God while denying foreordination?

    The Arminians (p. 66).

4. Can God elect someone to salvation who is not in fact saved?

   No. There must be a perfect correspondence between what He decrees and what occurs (p. 74).

5. What distinction does Vincent make with regard to the decrees of God?

   He distinguishes the general decrees, which includes the motion of every atom, and special decrees, which would include things like election and reprobation (p. 42).

6. What does not factor into God's decrees of election and reprobation?

   Neither the good works of the elect, not the evil works in the reprobate, were the basis for God's decision (p. 43).

7. In what two ways does God fulfill His decrees?

   In the works of creation and providence (p. 44).

8. According to Turretin, in what ways do the decrees of God not "inhere" in Him?

   They do not inhere in Him as accidents (v. 312).

9. Who denies the eternity of the decrees?

   The Socinians (p. 314).

10. Does God decree anything conditionally?

    No, contrary to the Socinians, Remonstrants (Arminians), and the Jesuits (p. 316).

Unit Four

1. What was the nature of the God who created the elements of the world out of nothing?

   This was done by the one God, who is Father, Son and Holy Spirit (p. 80).

2. What does Hodge mean by "absolute making"?

   He means creation from nothing, at the absolute beginning. The substance of matter must have had a beginning, as well as their present forms (p. 81).

3. What is meant by *creatio prima* and *creatio secunda*?

   The first refers to matter being created out of nothing. The second refers to God's sovereign arrangement of preexisting matter (p.82).

4. According to Vincent, what does the image of God not consist of?

   It does not consist of the outward and visible appearance of the body (p. 48).

5. What does it consist of?

   According to Vincent, it includes the universal and perfect rectitude of the whole soul (p. 48).

6. How does Vincent define a covenant?

   He says that it is a "mutual agreement and engagement, between two or more parties, to give or do something" (p. 51).

7. In what way does Turretin respond to the charge of fatalism?

   He responds by distinguishing what is meant by fate (p. 494ff).

8. What does he mean by "Christian fate"?

   He means the "series and order of causes depending on divine providence by which it produces its own effects" (p. 497).

9. How many things are under the providence of God?

   All things, from the greatest to the least (p. 498).

10. Are free and voluntary actions governed by providence?

   Absolutely (p. 500).

Unit Five

1. According to Hodge, in what moral state were our first parents created?

   They were created holy, yet capable of falling (p.105).

2. Since he could be tested and could fail, what sort of state was that?

   Adam was in a state of probation (p. 107).

3. When our first parents first sinned, what happened to them?

   They became dead in sins, and wholly corrupt (p. 109)

4. In what two ways was Adam the head of all mankind?

    He was both natural and federal head, Christ only excepted (p. 110).

5. What happens in true conviction of sin?

    We feel the burden, not only in what we have done, but also in what we are (p. 116).

6. What is meant by freedom of the will, according to Vincent?

    It is liberty to choose or to refuse, without external constraint (p. 54).

7. Where does Vincent say the law of God is to be found?

    It is written in the hearts of all men, but is most fully to be found in the Scriptures (p. 56).

8. Why did God forbid the tree of knowledge of good and evil?

    In order to try their obedience (p. 57).

9. Why was the Lord Jesus not entailed in the fall of Adam?

    Because He descended from Adam by an extraordinary generation, being born of a virgin (p. 59).

10. In what two ways were we all in Adam when he sinned?

    We were in him virtually, and we were in him representatively (p. 59).

Unit Six

1. How does Hodge describe man's faculty of self-determination?

    He calls it "inalienable" (p. 159).

2. What can an act of will from an unregenerate man not do?

    It cannot will toward salvation (p. 163).

3. What two kinds of call are distinguished by Hodge?

    An outward and inward effectual call (p. 168).

4. According to Vincent, was man ever able to keep the command of God perfectly?

    Adam could before the fall (p. 215).

5. How often do God's saints break the commandments of God?

   Daily (p. 219).

6. What is an ineffectual calling?

   A bare, external call (p. 90).

7. Does Turretin object to the use of the phrase free will?

   No, although the term should be taught in its right sense (p. 660).

8. Are necessity and free will ever inconsistent?

   Coactive and physical necessity are inconsistent with free will (p. 661).

9. Are the reprobate called by God?

   Yes, the reprobate are extended the external call of the gospel, but secondarily and indirectly (p. 504).

10. Why does God offer salvation to the reprobate?

    To prescribe to them their duty, to bless them by showing them the way of salvation, and to convict the stubborn and rebellious and give them no excuse (p. 505, 510).

Unit Seven

1. According to Hodge, who receives justification?

   All those and only those who are effectually called (p.179).

2. In what ways are justification and sanctification distinct graces?

   They are distinct in their nature, grounds, and ends (p. 181).

3. In what way is faith to be considered alone?

   It is unassociated with any other grace as the sole instrument of justification (p. 185).

4. According to Vincent, what are the two elements of justification?

   Pardon for sin, and a legal acceptation of us as righteous (p. 93).

5. In what ways are we to be considered children of God?

   By regeneration and by adoption (p.96).

6. What is the first distinction between justification and sanctification?

    Justification is outside us, while sanctification occurs within us (p. 98).

7. For Turretin, what is the basic statement of the question concerning justification?

    Whether or not justification is "precisely" a forensic act, or whether there is also a physical or moral infusion involved (II, p. 634).

8. Does Turretin believe justification to be eternal?

    No, not if speaking accurately (II, p. 683).

9. What is the difference between the chastisements that believers and unbelievers undergo?

    Believers receive corrective, disciplinary, or "medicinal" chastisements. For unbelievers, it is punitive (II, p.684).

10. When does justification occur?

    At the moment of effectual calling (II, p.684).

Unit Eight

1. According to Hodge, what is spontaneously exercised by all men?

    Faith in many thousands of its forms (p.203).

2. How does saving faith come about?

    It is wrought in our hearts by the Holy Ghost (p. 203).

3. What are the two components of saving faith according to Hodge?

    Assent to what Scripture teaches about the person, offices, and work of Christ, and trust in Christ alone for all that is involved in complete salvation (p. 205).

4. What is the essence of repentance?

    Hodge teaches that it is threefold—true hatred of sin, an actual turning from it, and a sincere purpose to walk with God (p. 210).

5. Is repentance a cause for pardon of sin?

    It is no cause whatever (p.214).

6. According to Vincent, what does God require of us that we may escape His wrath?

    Three things—faith in Jesus, repentance unto life, and diligent use of the means God has given us for appropriating the benefits of redemption (p. 224)

7. How does God work saving faith into the soul?

    Ordinarily through the hearing of the Word preached (p. 225).

8. Can any repent in the power of nature?

    No, because by nature we all have hearts of stone (p. 227).

9. What is hatred of sin?

    Hatred of sin is an inward deep loathing of it as the most odious thing in the world (p.231).

10. Is obedience required in the New Covenant?

    Yes, what is required is the new obedience of the gospel (p.232).

Unit Nine

1. According to Hodge, to whom does the promise of perseverance belong?

    To the true believer (p. 232).

2. What is not promised to the true believer?

    That he is exempt from the possibility of falling into grievous sin (p. 233).

3. Where is our certainty to be grounded?

    In the merits and intercession of Christ (p. 236).

4. How do unregenerate men frequently indulge themselves?

    Unfounded assurance of their own gracious condition (p. 239).

5. Is an infallible assurance of the very essence of faith?

    No, it is not (p. 243).

6. For Vincent, what is the first of five benefits that belong to justified persons?

    Assurance of God's love (p. 100).

7.   What is the fifth?

       Perseverance in grace to the end (p. 100).

8.   Who assuredly attains to the heavenly inheritance?

       All truly justified, adopted, and sanctified persons (p. 101).

9.   What is true of genuine believers who fall into sin?

       Though they may "fall into sin foully," and fall in some measure from grace, they cannot fall totally and finally from grace (p. 101).

10.   What is true of those who do fall totally and finally from grace?

       That they never had the sincerity which they professed (p. 101).

Unit Ten

1.   According to Hodge, in addition to being the natural head of the human race, what was Adam also?

       He was also the federal or covenant head (p. 248).

2.   How was the moral law summarily comprehended?

       In the Ten Commandments (p. 249).

3.   What is the Christian believer's relationship to the ceremonial law?

       Those laws cease to have any binding force (p. 254).

4.   According to Vincent, what is the rule for our obedience?

       God's revealed will (p. 110).

5.   Does the new covenant abolish the moral law?

       No—not at all (pp. 212–213).

6.   If the Ten Commandments are the summary of the whole moral law, what summarizes the Ten Commandments?

       The two great commandments (p. 114).

7.   Are all sins equally heinous?

       No (p. 219 ff.).

8.   According to Turretin, what distinction should be made in the use of the law?

Between absolute and relative (p. 137).

9. What is the difference between them?

   The absolute concerns the law in itself, while the relative concerns our relation to other men (p. 137).

10. What are the two ways man is obligated to keep the law?

    We owe both obedience proper and the penalty for disobedience (p. 140).

Unit Eleven

1. How does Hodge describe the regulative principle?

   He says it is a sin to neglect to worship God in the way prescribed, or to worship Him in a way not prescribed (p.270).

2. Why is it a sin to fail to worship God rightly?

   Because He has given us His Word, which is completely sufficient for us to know how to live, including how we must worship Him (p. 271).

3. What is Hodge's first objection to the worship of saints, angels or Mary?

   There is not a shadow of support for it in Scripture (p. 273).

4. What spirit should and should not attend Sabbath observance?

   It should not be marked by the spirit of the law, but rather by the spirit of the gospel (p. 283).

5. According to Vincent, how many parts are there in prayer?

   There are three—petition, confession, and thanksgiving (p. 266).

6. Why must we pray in the name of Christ?

   Because we could not be accepted by God otherwise (p. 268).

7. What special rule should direct our prayers?

   The Lord's prayer (p. 271).

8. According to Turretin, how many different kinds of Sabbath are there?

   Three—temporal, spiritual, and heavenly (II, p. 78).

9. What status does the fourth commandment have, according to Turretin?

   It is partly moral, partly ceremonial, which he identifies as the position of the orthodox (II, p.84).

10. What is the Lord's Day?

    It is the first day of the week (II, p.92).

Unit Twelve

1. Does Hodge believe that God has required any particular form of civil government for men?

   No, He has not (p. 294).

2. What is the point of civil government?

   The ultimate end is the glory of God, and the proximate end is the promotion of the public good (p. 295).

3. What should a Christian magistrate also seek?

   He should seek to promote piety as well as order (p. 295).

4. May Christian magistrates wage war?

   They may do so upon just and necessary occasions (p. 296).

5. What two civil arrangements does Hodge oppose?

   The papal, where the state submits to the church, and the Erastian, where the church submits to the state (p. 298).

6. Is marriage a religious contract only?

   No, it is a civil contract as well (p. 302).

7. Does Turretin believe that the laws of the Old Testament are abrogated?

   Some are, in some ways. He distinguishes (II, p. 166).

8. According to Turretin, does a believing magistrate have any responsibilities for the church?

   Yes, he does. Turretin says "he ought not to be excluded from all care of religion and sacred things" (III, p. 316).

9. What kind of right does the magistrate have in sacred things?

    A limited right, not an absolute right (III, p.319).

10. Can a magistrate compel men to faith?

    Not at all. Men should be drawn to faith by means of gospel promises (III, p.323).

Unit Thirteen

1. According to Hodge, who must acknowledge that the invisible Church is complete and full?

    Anyone who acknowledges either or both divine foreknowledge or foreordination (p. 311).

2. What kind of matter is the relative purity of the visible Church?

    It is a matter of degree (p. 316).

3. If Christ has appointed the pope or national sovereigns as heads over the Church, then what is disobedience to their authority? If He has not, then what is their claim?

    Treason against Christ if He has established them, and their usurpation is a blasphemous intrusion if He has not (p. 318).

4. How is union in the communion of saints accomplished?

    By the Holy Spirit and by faith (p. 324).

5. According to Vincent, why are the ordinances called the "ordinary means" for communicating the benefits of salvation to us?

    Because God is not bound to them, or limited by them, but the ordinances are the "most usual way and means of conversion and salvation" (p. 234).

6. How are the sacraments effectual means of salvation in a positive sense?

    By the blessing and presence of Christ, and by the working of the Spirit (p. 242).

7. What is signified by the outward sensible signs?

    Christ and the benefits of the New Covenant (p. 244).

8. According to Turretin, what is the "twofold" matter of a sacrament?

    The external and sensible aspect and the internal and intelligible (III, p. 339).

9. What is the "accidental end" of a certain use of the sacraments?

    The just condemnation of the wicked and the hypocrites (III, p.342).

10. What is the sin of "defect" in understanding the sacraments?

    Turretin refers to the error of the Socinians, who hold that the sacraments are "bare signs" and "mere figures." Romanists and Lutherans falsely charge the Reformed with this error (III, pp.361–362).

Unit Fourteen

1. According to Hodge, what kind of action is the action of baptism?

    It is an action of washing, the mode being a matter of indifference (p.340)

2. Were infants members of the church in the older covenant?

    Yes, they were circumcised upon the faith of their parents (p. 347).

3. What kind of kingdom is the church?

    It is a theocratic kingdom (p. 367).

4. Who will be present at the last day of judgment?

    The entire human race, encompassing each generation, each individual appearing before God in the completeness of his reintegrated person, both soul and body (p. 391).

5. According to Vincent, what does the water of baptism signify?

    It signifies the blood of Jesus Christ (p. 246).

6. Why does Vincent think the inclusion of infants in the Old Testament was never taken away or removed?

    Because if they were excluded, it would have been mentioned somewhere (p. 251).

7. Where do Christians go when they die?

    They go to their Father's house in Heaven (p. 103)

8. According to Turretin, how are infants included in the Great Commission?

   The genus nations includes the species infants (III, p. 415).

9. What word is used to describe the sacrament of the Supper most frequently?

   The word mystery (III, p.426).

10. What is the first reason for church discipline?

   Turretin refers to the need to remove those named among Christians who lead a disgraceful and wicked life (III, p.293).

Made in the USA
Middletown, DE
06 July 2024

56755673R00146